Eddie

Copyright © 2017 by Michael K. Gantt
MKGANTT.COM PUBLICATIONS
Brattleboro, Vermont

This book is dedicated to our wonderful basket of friends who have stood with us, wept with us, laughed with us, and walked with us for so very many years. It is especially dedicated to so many of you who followed us, laughed and cried with us, and prayed with us on our little adventure with Cousin Eddie, our antique motor home who, without any warning at all, inserted himself into our crazy family and became one of us.

While the events recorded here are encapsulated in a very brief month, I have realized that they define who we have been for our entire lives.

Eddie

Adventures with a 41-Year Old RV and the Lessons He Taught Us

---

M.K. Gantt

Foreword

Sometimes you plan a vacation and it turns into an adventure. *Sometimes* the most unlikely characters become the hero of your story. The unlikely hero of our story is a 41-year old motor home that was christened with the name "Cousin Eddie."

I always thought my first published book would be a careful exposition of the Scriptures, leading many brethren to a deeper and fuller walk with Christ. Instead, what we have here is a record of the consequences of what could be considered a poor decision.

This little book is written in response to requests from friends all over America who followed our daily Facebook posts while on vacation in September of 2017. During a series of misadventures, we found that we were providing many people with some measure of enjoyment, and during these misadventures I discovered that God was reinforcing some important truths in my own life.

All in all, it was a wonderful experience as Barbara and I got to spend more time together in a single stretch than we had in many years. Combine two recent retirees, 23 children and grandchildren, a tornado and two hurricanes, close to 3000 of highway with a 41-year-old motor home named "Cousin Eddie," and what could go wrong?

Please, allow me to expound upon that just a bit.

Prologue

On September 5, 2017, my wife Barbara and I embarked upon a much-anticipated road trip from Vermont to Florida and back. Our itinerary included driving our 41-year old motor home to Orlando, Florida and Disney World where we would be joined by our children and grandchildren. During the next couple of weeks our extended family; *all 25 of us,* converged on the Magic Kingdom and to say we had a great time would be a significant understatement.

Throughout our journey to Florida and back, Barbara and I had the opportunity to spend some great days together, something we hadn't been able to do in a long, long time. As events unfolded, not only did we realize that our vacation was turning into a real-life adventure; a mix of scary moments stirred in with some moments of incredible hilarity and through it all, my best friend, Jesus allowed me to realize that He was teaching us some great lessons.

The response to our regular trip updates posted on Facebook was very enthusiastic. Many of our friends *(and a bunch of people I've never heard of before)*, cheered us on and repeatedly suggested that I ought to "write a book." What follows is a compilation of those adventures and the lessons we learned from them. However, to fully appreciate how all of this came to pass one must first hear the backstory or, *how it all began.*

1 | Cousin Eddie

Sometimes you plan a vacation and it turns into an adventure. Sometimes the most unlikely characters become the hero of your story. The unlikely hero of our story is a 41-year-old motor home who became known as "Cousin Eddie."

Our oldest son Bryan and our youngest girl Abigail love everything Disney. The two of them hatched a plan for a family vacation to Disney World in Florida to coincide with our retirement. I served as Pastor of Agape Christian Fellowship for just about 37 years and my wife operated a Registered Daycare in our home for the better part of 35 years. More than a year before, I had stepped away from the role of lead pastor, handing those responsibilities over to my son, Michael Bryan. In July of 2017 my wife officially closed the doors of her daycare. About two years earlier, the kids began planning our Disney trip which became known as the "Great Gantt/Stires Family Vacation."

As you might imagine, the coordination of a vacation for some 25 people to travel to Florida from Vermont and spend the better part of two weeks at Disney World is no small feat. Securing vacation times, making travel arrangements, tickets and housing, and a thousand other details must be synchronized to perfection. But, they did it. I wouldn't say "to perfection," but they managed to pull it off. Our dates were set, time off from work was secured, money was saved, condos were reserved, flight plans, rental cars, right down to the "fast passes" so we could all ride on the more exciting rides together - perfectly planned to come off without a hitch; *right in the middle of hurricane season.* Remember that last part as it will become very important to our story.

In the original plan, the kids were all going to drive down to Florida. I knew that at our age, Barbara and I would have no interest in jumping in a van and driving the more than 1200 miles straight through to Florida. *In fact, these days, my car pulls into the first motel it sees after the sun goes down.* As our plans progressed, the kids realized that flying would be more cost effective than driving and everyone made airline reservations. That is, everyone except Barbara and I. You see, Barbara refuses to fly. I fail to understand how she has managed to ride in a car with me for the past 50 years or so and yet fears flying. Most people think that riding in a car with me and flying are pretty much the same thing. The only way I could get Barb on a plane is to get her drunk - and since we are both teetotalers, that's not an option either.

We decided we were going to purchase a pop-up camper to tow behind our SUV. We would leave a couple of weeks ahead of the kids and enjoy an easy, meandering drive down the east coast to Florida, arriving about the same time as the kids were scheduled to fly in. It was a good plan, a sensible plan; but as I watched the local papers, scoured Craigslist, and the online swap shops in our area I simply could not find a pop up camper that met our rigid specifications: **good condition, low price.** I don't think I've mentioned that my wife is very frugal. Now, within the family we use words like *cheap* or *tight* but since my wife might read this, and she is after all, Scotch/Irish, I have chosen to use the word *frugal.* Let it suffice to say that when she squeezes a nickel - two dimes pop out.

One day, I observed my youngest son chatting online with a friend about a motor home he had purchased. His description was that it was "pretty old" but in great shape. He had plans for fixing it up and doing some travel in it. As it turns out, he and his girlfriend decided to get married and *ONE* of them decided that they needed the cash more than they needed a beat up old RV, and it had to be sold. From the tone of the conversation, I was sure that it wasn't he who made that decision. So, in a typical male reaction, I jumped in on the conversation and said, *"I'd like to see this RV. It sounds JUST like what I'm looking for."*

Now, it wasn't just what we were looking for - *not at all.* But, for my very male brain make the leap from pop-up trailer to a full grown 30-foot RV Motorhome with a full bath, refrigerator, gas stove, rooftop air conditioner, AND a 440-cubic inch muscle car engine with matching captain's chairs was such an easy transition to make. *Why, it's practically the same thing - right?*

Long story short: A deal was struck. Hands were shaken. Money was exchanged and soon my brand new 1976 Cruise Air Motor Home on a Dodge frame, red and white stripes, chrome mirrors, and 440 cubic inches of gas loving power was sitting in my driveway. *What could go wrong?*

Somewhere there is a scripture verse that says, "There is a way that seems right to a man, but the end thereof is destruction."

A few days later, my son Andrew pulled into our driveway. He got out of his car and stood, hands on hips, looking at my new acquisition. After a long and concentrated stare, a little smile began to form in the corners of his mouth as quietly; almost reverently, he whispered, *"Cousin Eddie."*

Now, for those who might not grasp the implications of such a pronouncement, you need to watch Chevy Chase in his movie, **CHRISTMAS VACATION**. For Clark Griswold, vacations have a way of morphing from warm family experiences to chaotic disasters of epic proportions. In **CHRISTMAS VACATION**, the chaotic disaster arrives in the form of his cousin Eddie, who shows up at the Griswold home in a beat up old Winnebago motor home.

Eddie, played by character actor and all around goof up Randy Quaid, roars into the picture single handedly bringing with him an unmitigated disaster upon the Griswold family Christmas.

"That's an ARRR-VEEE!"

As soon as Andrew breathed those words we both began to howl with laughter. I realized he was exactly right. That antique "arrr-vee" sitting in my driveway looked hauntingly like the rolling chaos from the movie and hence, *Cousin Eddie was born.* In fact, for Christmas I was given a five-foot decal with the words, **Cousin Eddie,** a leather bombardier's hat, a woman's white half bathrobe, a can of Pabst Blue Ribbon Beer and instructions that I should wear it every time I drained the holding tank. (Sorry, you gotta to watch the movie to appreciate this image).

The whole scene evoked eerie similarities to a cinematic disaster of Titanic proportions and yet, I couldn't see it.

A tarp was placed over Eddie for the winter and in the spring the preparations began as the date approached for the Great Gantt/Stires Family Vacation. I won't bore you with the entire list of repairs and restoration that had to take place before we could leave, but given that Eddie was 41 years old, you might surmise there were a few. Eddie sat proudly in our driveway for months as I patched, painted, repaired, replaced, added, fixed, tweaked, wired, waxed and polished.

I installed a DVD player and a 40" flat screen television with a ROKU unit so that when we had access to the internet we could enjoy the best in TV entertainment. I removed the old gas/electric fridge and replaced it with a new, electric fridge. We found a spot for our Keurig coffee maker and I found and replaced the control switch for the Air Conditioner. The old, stainless steel gas stove and oven was rusted so I sanded it down and painted it with a pristine white high heat enamel. I was turning Eddie into a veritable palace - fit for a King and his Queen.

I cheerfully greeted our neighbors as they walked by our drive on their morning constitutional, often stopping for a stare, a shake of the head and a giggle. When I would explain that my wife and I had retired and we were going to travel from Vermont to Florida and back the snickers would turn into howls of laughter, but I remained undaunted, unaffected, and undeterred by their ridicule. A pastor friend who lives up the street suggested personal counseling and the suggestion that Eddie might not even make it to Massachusetts, let alone Florida. I started getting anonymous messages on Facebook, (they're not truly anonymous, but everybody seems to think they are since you can't see them typing), suggesting that they had always suspected I was crazy and now, had confirmation. People offered Barbara safe housing if she needed a haven to which she could flee.

Undaunted, the preparations for our great adventure continued as we stocked in food supplies. We bought canned beans and beanie-weenies, Dinty Moore Beef Stew, Vienna Sausages, various soups, mac and cheese. We stocked Eddie with bottled water and sodas. We shelved towels and sheets and blankets, put dishes in the cupboards, filled up the propane tank, mounted new tires, an oil change and a myriad of other preparations.

In the weeks prior to our departure I did experience several setbacks. I inexplicably lost power in one entire circuit of interior lights, the electronic fuel tank valve that allows you to switch between gas tanks stopped working and after countless hours lying on my back trying to sort out what the matter might be I was forced to install a manual valve that would require stopping the RV and getting out on the side of the road and manually switch from one tank to the other. The fuel gauges stopped working, the dashboard instruments ceased to function, and the wiring to the trailer hitch fell off. The night before our departure the emergency brake froze up, necessitating some last minute repairs.

We planned to tow a car behind Eddie so that when we were parked in a campground we would be able to enjoy the surrounding areas while leaving Eddie safely parked and hooked up to utilities. (Secretly, but unspoken, it was also a ride home just in case the worst happened.) I borrowed a tow dolly from a friend. I got a good deal from a friend and purchased a 2001 VW Jetta with a standard shift that would be perfect for towing.

Finally, the time of our departure was at hand. The great adventure was about to commence. Everything was ready. Food shelves were stocked, blankets and sheets, clothing in our closets, gas in the tanks, lights were working, fridge was working. I had (wisely) joined AAA with an RV package, *just in case*. I enrolled in the EZ Pass program so we could roll right through toll booths.

You know, the male psyche is an amazing thing to consider. *If I had been honest* I would have admitted that in the weeks leading up to this grand adventure I would lay awake at night, fearfully imagining all the things that could and probably would go wrong. In my mind I saw images of fiery crashes in the mountains of Virginia. Because I am so familiar with the roads in that area well, there were hills that I secretly was sure Eddie would never be able to climb towing that trailer and car.

There was one hill, at Fancy Gap, just at the Virginia/North Carolina border; a steep 12-mile downhill grade, where I imagined the brakes failing and us careening down that hill. In my mind's eye, I could see us screaming down that mountain pass, completely out of control, no brakes and no control. I spent sleepless nights trying to remember where all the "escape ramps" were.

Just a few weeks before we were to leave, a friend and his son in North Carolina died horribly in a fiery crash in their RV; an event which only fueled my dark fantasies. One nightmarish imagination after another tormented me for weeks, and I would suffer in silence because I didn't want to admit my secret: I was afraid that I had made a stupid decision and the result would be putting my wife and myself in danger. In more than one midnight hour I would decide, *"That's it - I'm calling the whole thing off!"* Then, morning would come and I would start another day outwardly cheerful and confident, but inwardly terrified that I was going to kill us both. In my mind, I understood that the fears were greatly exaggerated and spiritual rather than real, and yet, I wrestled with those demons for weeks, living in fear and unable to ask for help.

I was so anxious that I had to start taking meds again for my ulcer because of the worry. I would lay in bed at night, doubled up in pain because of all the acid my troubled stomach was producing. The greatest pain was that my ego would not allow me to share my concerns with my wife or my friends. It seemed for a while like this great adventure was going to get the best of me without ever leaving the driveway.

You know, it's not a sin to be fearful. Sin comes when we allow our fears to continue to have power over us. When Jehoshaphat learned that a great, allied army was approaching Judah, he was afraid.

After this the Moabites and Ammonites, and with them some of the Meunites, [a] came against Jehoshaphat for battle. Some men came and told Jehoshaphat, "A great multitude is coming against

13

*you from Edom, from beyond the sea; and, behold, they are in Hazazon-tamar" (that is, Engedi). Then **Jehoshaphat was afraid and set his face to seek the Lord,** and proclaimed a fast throughout all Judah. And Judah assembled to seek help from the Lord; from all the cities of Judah they came to seek the Lord.* [2 Chronicles 20:1-4 ESV]

I didn't intend to write a book about our adventures. I just thought it would be fun to chronicle our trip for the enjoyment of our friends and family. However, so many have suggested that I should compile our adventures in one place for others to enjoy. As I have written down some of the hilarious and fun things that happened along our way, I also realized that God was also teaching me, or at least reminding me, of some important spiritual lessons.

I have always admired Jehoshaphat the King because his life has taught me two important things:

1. **It's alright, even normal, to be afraid.** The man who says he is never afraid is either a fool or a liar. Men are particularly vulnerable to fear when they realize that they are facing a situation that is out of their control. I'm not particularly given to fear. I travel all over the world and have been in some pretty dicey situations and could always manage or at least stare down my fears. The greatest fear for me is that fear that grips me in the dark of the night, in my imagination - because that fear is a powerful, often irrational fear, involving matters that I can't get my hands on. Jehoshaphat was afraid - and right well he should have been because he was facing an army that was so much stronger than the armies of Judah. He was facing an enemy that he could not defeat.

2. **When I am afraid I need to do two things**. *First*, I need to set my face to seek the Lord. I need to be like Jehoshaphat and admit to the Lord that I am facing something that is too big for me, or something that I can't see anyway of defeating, or as it was with me - something spiritual, darkly supernatural that was defeating me because it was defeating me in my mind, in the spiritual realm. Jehoshaphat set himself to seek help from God because his fears. *Secondly,* I need to swallow my pride and find someone who can stand with me in my fears. I need to find someone who can pray with me. Jehoshaphat called all the people of Judah together and realizing that all of them together could not defeat the enemy that was coming, they sought God's help together.

Of course, the other thing I learned in all of this is that I am completely inept at hiding anything from my wife. I spent weeks wearing the manly bravado mantle - *and fooling no one.*

As I chronicled our trip via Facebook posts I could share with our friends and family our adventures. It turns out that my fears were completely unfounded, hugely overblown and we had a month together that was way beyond wonderful. However, while I was sharing all our fun, I realized that God was reminding me of some wonderful truths along the way. This is not written with any mind to being "preachy" or some seminal theological statement. But, I have realized as I nursed this huge, gas guzzling hog of a motor home to Florida and back, that God was using Eddie to remind me of a lot of little nuggets of encouragement that sometimes are just as important as the deep theological truths we seek to understand.

And for many of us - *Eddie has become just another member of our crazy family.*

15

2 | First Log Entry

September 5, 2017

(Spoiler alert – some of the narrative in this chapter might sound a hair repetitive because it is taken from almost directly from my Facebook post on the first day of our journey.)

After months of anticipation and preparation our great adventure has begun. We finally departed Brattleboro at around 8:00 am this morning. The final hours before departure were a bit of a challenge.

Thanks to the generosity of my friend Travis Mitchell we have a tow dolly with which to tow our little red Jetta. I brought the dolly home night before last and thought that probably I should just do a test to make sure the dolly was going to work. I got the VW in place and loaded it onto the dolly. It drove up the ramp and onto the dolly easily. Beautiful. Satisfied that all was well, I backed the VW off the dolly and as I did, I heard something scraping. I got out to see what it was only to find the entire front bumper of the VW laying on the ground. The bottom skirt of the bumper was too low and caught on an edge of the dolly - pulled the whole thing off.

I stuck my head in the back door and spoke to Barbara, suggesting that she should go ahead and eat supper without me as I picked up my tool box, hooked up a set of work lights and spent the next two hours re-attaching the bumper. I had to make some minor modifications on it to insure it wouldn't catch again. The good thing is I am still smiling. I didn't yell, I didn't shoot it, and *I didn't cuss.* That's one win for me. *Aha!*

Last night, in preparation for our morning departure I fired up Eddie's engine to move it forward a bit in the driveway, getting into position to hitch up the tow dolly and load up the car.

Climbed in.
Shut the door.
Put in the key.
Fired up the engine.
All systems go.
Except . . . when I eased the transmission into drive - Eddie wouldn't move.
I mean wouldn't budge.

I slid the gear selector into reverse. Wouldn't budge. Wheels frozen. I put it back into Drive and gave it some EXTRA accelerator and Eddie did, grudgingly, move forward screeching like I was running over a flock of buzzards. It was at that moment that after months of functioning perfectly; I realized that the emergency brake was frozen solid.

I cussed.

There, I've admitted it. Now everyone knows that there is a point to which I can be dragged where words come out of my mouth that I didn't want any of you to know were in there. I wish they weren't there. I detest profane language and yet, it lurks within my heart always on the lookout for an escape route. I usually keep them chained up and out of sight, but last night a couple of the little guys escaped. It will cheer your heart to know that they have all been captured and returned to their cells. In the meantime, I called my good friend Tim Mitchell who has helped me so much in getting Eddie ready to go. Bless his heart, he got up from the supper table and came over to the house. Out came the tool box. Out came the work lights and into the dark of the night Tim and I wrestled with that brake. A final solution was arrived at when from under Eddie's belly Tim yelled out, "Do you have a hack saw?"

I couldn't find my hack saw, but I did locate my reciprocating saw *and Eddie no longer has an emergency brake.*

All that being said, our 41-year-old RV Motor Home, christened by my children as "Cousin Eddie" performed with class today as we drove from Brattleboro to our first stop: Red Run RV Park in Ephrata, PA. Eddie *performed* well. However, we did learn something about him that we had suspected, and about which we had been warned but could not confirm until we had actually travelled some distance with him.

Eddie has a drinking problem. He has a voracious appetite for gasoline. The best estimation I can make at this point is that we are getting around 4.8 miles to the gallon.

We arrived at the Red Run Campground in Ephrata at around 4:00 p.m. in the afternoon. We registered, found our spot and began to attach the hoses and electrical hook-up. It had rained a bit on the way in, just a drizzle, but overall it was a lovely late afternoon. I was working outside while Barbara was working inside, preparing for our three day stay in Amish country. I had just hooked up the electrical when I heard a sound that made me think we might be camped on the landing approach for some Amish airport. I turned around, expecting to see a jumbo jet glide over our heads. Instead, I saw trees bending and twisting toward the ground. Limbs and whole trees went flying in every direction. I thought, *"This could be a good time to step in for a cup of coffee."*

We sat inside as the RV rocked back and forth, feeling more like a boat at sea than a motor home. We watched as leaves were

18

stripped from trees and since we were parked under a beautiful butternut tree, just chock full of butternuts, it sounded like we had come under fire from a machine gun as the nuts rained down upon us. From inside you could hear the crack and crash of limbs snapping and trees falling.

I had been admiring a beautiful 48-foot motor home that had pulled in right behind us. It was gorgeous; a beautiful example of modern technology -- all the bells and whistles. Earlier, as it glided smoothly by Eddie on its way to their own parking spot, I felt just a little envy. Not much, just a little. Now, as I looked out the window in their direction I realized that stretched out across the stern of that beautiful, brand-new land boat was a fifty-foot butternut tree. The wind had pulled it right up by the roots and dropped it right over the back of that motor home, crushing it to the ground. I feared what we would find. I saw the campground manager fly over in his truck as other workers ran to the site. I could see quite a crowd gathered and that, thankfully, the owners were o.k. I elected for time being to stay out of the way.

I stepped outside for a moment, when I saw that just a few spaces down from us another camper had been struck by a falling tree and just a way over from us there was a large tent with a tree branch sticking right through it -- top to bottom. Fortunately, the tent dwellers were not home at the time. The little creek that runs through the campground was now a raging torrent, ready to breach its banks. We later found out that several tornadoes had touched down in the area and though we hadn't seen a funnel, we certainly had felt its power.

Eddie survived without a scratch. But then I thought - *"Without a scratch? How would you know?"*

I unloaded the VW so that Barb and I could drive into Lancaster for dinner. By the time we got back things had calmed down considerably. We will remain here until Friday morning. Keep us in your prayers as we meander down through the mountains of Virginia on Friday remembering that the bulk of our vacation and the whole of everyone else's in the family is in Florida which now is directly in the sights of hurricane Irma. This appears to be a very strong storm that will hit the southern coast of Florida sometime on Sunday.

Not for the sake of our vacation, but for the sake of the lives of those in Irma's path, please make urgent prayer on their behalf. May God in His mercy blow Irma out to sea and spare Floridians a similar fate as struck Houston.

As for Barbara and I, we are safely tucked into the innards of Cousin Eddie as a hard rain falls on the roof. Barb is having a little asthma attack tonight. Please pray for quick relief. *More later*

Ephrata Day 2

Barb and I are hunkered down in PA at our campground. Last night just after we arrived and as we were setting up, tornadoes touched down all over Lancaster Country. We are not sure about our location because we never actually saw a funnel, but at the very least we experienced a powerful microburst which destroyed several RV's and tents; one which had a huge a tree fall right through it. Fortunately, the folks that lived there were in the front. If it had occurred in the nighttime they would most surely have been killed.

We thought we had escaped unscathed. We were wrong. During the night, it rained-hard. I am not sure what time it was but I was awakened by the sound of dripping water; not outside but inside and not drip-drip but slosh-slosh. I got up quietly so as not to disturb Barb and shined my flashlight toward the sound of the dripping water. To my dismay I saw that in fact, we had developed a large leak or leaks and water was pouring out of the front cabinet over the Captain's chairs and onto the table between them. The table was literally wallowing in water and right in the center of the wallowing water was my IPhone - also wallowing in water. *I didn't cuss.* However, my groans did wake Barbara up.

When morning came, I discovered that several branches had fallen, piercing the rubberized roof material with some small holes. We awakened today with several sizable leaks, now being serviced by our kitchen pots. Climbing up on the roof, I discovered that it has some "low" spots where water gathers and stands and that those low spots coincide with the areas damaged by falling debris. Consequently, I have been on the roof several times today sweeping off the standing water trying to keep the damage on the inside to a minimum. It is supposed to be better weather tomorrow so I can get up there, dry things off and spray some magic Flex Seal in hopes of stemming the flow. I went inside to ask Barb what she was going to cook for dinner. She just looked woefully around the room, observing that every cooking utensil we own is currently catching water and said, *"I think we'll be going out for lunch.*

We drove into New Holland to the Mennonite second hand store, which is one of Barb's favorite places to shop. She shopped and I found a good book and read. Renuzit shops have several locations around Lancaster County. They are part of the mission arm of the Mennonite Church. These are beautiful stores that sell everything from books, to clothing, to furniture (they even deliver) and decor items. The shops are manned entirely by volunteers. They are clean, expertly organized, and very reasonably priced and ALL proceeds go to worldwide missions and relief efforts of the Mennonite Church. They stand in stark contrast to many of the second-hand shops we often see which are dark, poorly organized affairs which offer not so appealing items. Renuzit shops are one of our favorite stops in Lancaster County.

Later in the day we visited another of my treasured spots in Lancaster County: **The Bird-in-Hand Farmer's Market**. You must not visit Amish country without visiting this delightful place. They are open every week from Wednesday through Saturday and you can find the most wonderful meats, vegetables, fudge, crafts, dips, popcorns, coffees, leather goods, bulk food items, and of course, my personal favorite — *hot dogs*.

We of course, finished our day off in Lancaster at **The Bird-in-Hand Family Restaurant** in Bird-in-Hand. Well known, not only for their excellent food, they also have an excellent dinner theater as well. Great place to eat and shop, and be entertained.

If we believe the weather reports, IRMA is getting ready to blow the lid off our vacation plans. We're watching very carefully the weather, but if things don't change drastically, Bryan and his family won't get out on schedule, and we won't make it in time for our current reservations. Of course, we are praying on lots of fronts that in His mercy God will steer the storm back out to sea. (He does those kinds of things from time to time). I'm not so worried about our vacation as I am for the people in Florida. Vacations can be rescheduled - *lives cannot.*

As I sit here in the darkness, listening to drip, drip, drip into my soup pot, I am grateful for the goodness of God and I am reminded over and over that nothing in the universe, on this planet, and nothing in our lives happens without the permission of the Hand of Providence. We are kept in Him and in Him we trust. From the standpoint of the flesh, it can be discouraging when things don't go the way we plan, but in Him everything is perfectly timed; *whether we can see it or not.*

I am constrained to give thanks to God for all things and in all things and to recognize that our nation and our world face far greater and far darker issues than interrupted vacation plans. Hundreds of thousands of lives are living in chaos in Houston, millions of lives lie in the path of another giant storm, and nuclear war could be on the horizon; not to mention a rift in the heart of America that could throw us into a civil war.

Let us not complain to God about our minor delays and inconvenience, but rejoice that if we are His children, our lives are etched in the palm of His hand and kept in the cleft of the Rock who is Jesus - our Helper, our Provider, and our Savior. The little disruptions that come into our lives pale in comparison to the knowledge that we are hidden in Him and his purposes are always for good. All my children and grandchildren will testify to the number of times I have said to them, "The Word of God is NEVER not true."

Romans 8:28 says, *"All things work together for good to them that love God and are called by his purpose."* This word is ALWAYS true and no matter what it is never NOT true. Hold on to that truth with confidence and no matter what, let your voice be lifted in praise before all men everywhere.

So many who live in darkness, blame God when bad things happen. They believe that if God were truly good, nothing bad would ever happen. Sadly, many of us who claim to know Christ and who claim to love God tend to respond in the same way as those who live in darkness. When bad things happen we get discouraged and we cease to praise Him as if in some way He has treated us unfairly or has failed to protect us as He ought. God is good all the time and He is not the author of the evil that transpires in our world. This is the result of the wickedness and rebellion of man, and that when man fell, all of creation fell with him. The Scriptures declare that *"the rain falls upon the just and the unjust."* The fact that I am a Christ-follower does not mean that I will not suffer. It is in fact, how I respond to bad things; whether a tornado or a frozen emergency brake that is supposed to set us apart from those who live in darkness.

I spoke this morning to a husband and wife who had just retired and moved PERMANENTLY into their new RV as they sadly picked through the ruins of their new home; completely destroyed in an instant by a falling tree in a freak storm, *"You have lost nothing that cannot be replaced, and the things that are of true value you still have. Do not mourn the loss of the temporary in the face of holding to that which is forever."*

Be blessed my friends in all things always. Do not murmur, do not complain, do not fret over the loss of temporary things; do not worry but put your trust in Him who can keep you in all circumstances and will show Himself strong to those who put their trust in Him.

NOTE; Every vacation we've ever taken has turned into an adventure. I don't know why I should expect that this one should be any different. Tomorrow, we're going to drive down into the Virginia mountains and hold up there until IRMA decides what she is going to do.

3 | Virginia

We had a great day yesterday, roaming around Lancaster County shopping and eating and seeing the sights. The rain finally stopped and I could get up onto the roof of Cousin Eddie and effect repairs caused by the little tornado that ripped through our RV park within 15 minutes of our arrival. We bought some gifts, went to our favorite Dutch Smorgasbord, and spent several hours at the Bird-in-Hand Farmer's Market.

We got up moderately early, packed up the RV, loaded the car onto the tow dolly as we headed out to Virginia where our adventure tonight finds us in the parking lot of Walmart in Harrisonburg, VA. I have the feeling that many who are following us are going to be disappointed on the days when nothing falls off or breaks. I am in hopes that you will rejoice with us when things go well as much as you laugh at us when something falls off. *Nothing fell off today.*

For years as we have traveled this same road between New England and our home in North Carolina we have made White's Truck Stop in Steele's Tavern VA a regular stop. It has always been a busy and fun place to spend a while resting. I pushed Eddie hard today to get here because both Barbara and I thought it would be fun to stop there again.

We finally made it to White's Truck Stop late this afternoon. It's a LOT BIGGER than either of us remember it. It is like a shopping mall now with all sorts of places to shop and eat. We did eat at the Iron Skillet Restaurant and then headed back out to the quiet spot on the back of the lot where we had parked Eddie, and had thoughts of spending the night. Since we are not staying in Virginia, we didn't want to rent a campsite and go through all the bother of hooking up utilities just to pull out early in the morning.

As we walked across the huge asphalt parking lot I remarked to Barbara, *"I'm afraid it's going to be hot tonight but the sun will go down soon and it should cool down a bit."* Now, when went into the restaurant to eat, we left Eddie in a remote corner of the lot in hopes that it might not be too, too busy with truck traffic. When we got back to our spot, we couldn't even find Eddie. I thought, *"He must have been stolen."* And then I thought, *"Who in the world is THAT desperate? Let's keep looking".*

We finally found him, poor little guy, buried in the midst of a yard full of monster trucks. He looked like a midget amid giants. A truck had pulled in on either side of us, so close that we could barely get the door open and wouldn't you know it, they were both "refers," or refrigerated trucks that have a separate engine for their freezers mounted on the front of the trailer and they run constantly - like as in all night, as in right outside my window; both windows in fact. *We tried.* We tried to settle in; but it was unbearably hot and because we weren't hooked up to an electrical supply, we couldn't run our own air conditioner. In addition to their refrigerator gasoline engines running, both drivers were bed down for the night in their diesel tractors with their engines running so they could run their air conditioners.

As we sat there between those two trucks with our little camper humming from the vibration of our neighbors, I was reminded of a stop we made years ago while traveling with our two older children, Bryan and Robyn. We were traveling in an itinerant ministry at the time and money was scarce. At times, we had to stay in some pretty humble housing. We had stopped in Wind Gap, PA at a small, travelers rest motel; nothing fancy, not expensive. When we checked into our room, our daughter Robyn was beset by curiosity at the fact that our beds had coin slots attached to the headboards. She was delighted by the fact that when you put a quarter into the slot, the entire bed would vibrate. It was noisy and not at all relaxing, but Robyn found it to be an item of immense delight. For months, everywhere we could go Robyn would announce to all who would listen, "We stayed in this hotel and we had a VIBRATOR in our room!"

I was lying on a bunk reading when I sat up, grabbed my phone, and started a search on the internet. Barb put down her book and said, "You had better be looking for some place else to stay." She was yelling, not because she was mad, but parked where we were, it was the only way to hear one another. *I was, and I did.* I didn't enjoy a room with a vibrator back then, and I wasn't enjoying it now.

We backtracked north to the town of Harrisonburg, where we could park at this lovely Walmart. It is blissfully quiet and the area of the parking lot where we are located looks an awful lot like an RV park, as there are at least 6 other units here. (Though none are as unique as our Cousin Eddie. We stand alone. I'm sure that some quite as unique as our Eddie). Our Walmart neighbors are looking out the window of their units feeling an awful lot like Clark Griswold right now.

We left Ephrata, PA this morning and press on, determined to have our "great adventure" whether we make it to Florida or not. We've decided that it doesn't matter - we are together, we are safe, we are having a good time (except when I have stop for gas - there is a lot of crying then as Eddie is getting NOT QUITE 5 miles to the gallon in these mountains pulling a car behind.).

Thanks to all who have expressed concerns for our safety. Be assured that we are carefully watching the weather and tracking the storm all the way. We may be crazy, but we're not stupid. Though some of our friends might disagree.

In the meantime, I'm learning a lot about myself. Not all of what I am learning is good, but it is all helpful. I have learned that though I declare my trust in God, my flesh is determined to war with me in this matter. I have worried about our vehicle, about the weather, and about the traffic. I lay in bed one night with almost no sleep, convinced we were going to crash into a fiery heap by the side of the road. When I worry, I get grumpy and sullen. I don't speak to Barbara (who is having a great time by the way) as I should and I frustrate her because I'm worried about so many things. Should we go on, should we go home, should we, should we - and then in the middle of all the gnashing of teeth I declare, *"Lord, I trust you!"* Except for the fact that I don't, not really. Too much of the time I trust more in ME than I do in HIM.

The book of Galatians declares that the flesh is always resisting the spirit, and in the same way the spirit is trying to hold down the work of the flesh. We are all going to have moments when it seems like the flesh; our fears, our worries, our anxieties will get the best of us. We must always shout above the screeching and complaining of our flesh with the voice of command, "Bless the Lord O my soul, and all that is within me, bless His Holy Name." Fear and worry only win when they cause us to draw back and to retreat.

I have never been one to yield to fear or to draw back and I'm thinking I am not going to start at this stage of my life. However, I would not be honest if I didn't mention that sometimes my spirit must shout louder than my flesh and declare, *" I lift up my eyes to the hills. From where does my help come? My help comes from the LORD, who made heaven and earth. "* (Psalm 137:1-2 ESV)

Remember that when warriors charge into battle, they shout. When the command is given in every movie you've ever seen depicts soldiers charging the enemy with determined faces and mighty shouts.

As Joshua and the children of Israel stood around the walls of Jericho, they blew the trumpet and lifted a mighty shout. With Gideon also, when the command was given the 300 men smashed their pitchers, blew their trumpets and shouted, *"The sword of the Lord and Gideon!"* The enemy seems to be routed as much by fearsome shouts as he is by terrible weapons.

Morning has come and we are again on the road. With each mile that passed as we drove from Pennsylvania down through the hills of Virginia we were coming closer to two of the greatest concerns I had anticipated for weeks: Christiansburg and Fancy Gap.

From the Ironto exit, just south of Salem, Virginia to Christiansburg there is a long, grinding pull of almost 15 miles. Over the years I have traveled that road, I have seen trucks, campers, and automobiles pulled over to the side; broken and wounded, great billows of steam rising from underneath their hoods. It was hot and I was driving a 41-year-old box on wheels, dragging an extra 2500 pounds behind on a tow dolly. For months, the doubts had been growing. Could Eddie make that climb to Christiansburg or were we going to be yet another sad victim on the side of the road?

As the Exit Sign for Ironto flew past I shouted, *"Come on Eddieeeeee - Let's do this!"* Barbara must have picked up on my anxiety because she began to pray. I pulled into the "slow traffic lane" expecting the inevitable groans and whines to begin as Eddie confronted this daunting climb. Much to my surprise - - and great delight -- Eddie settled into a smooth 48 mph climb. The temperature gauge rose to 240 degrees and stopped, holding steady, as Eddie bravely climbed.

I smiled as we passed long haul trucks struggling to make the pull to Christiansburg or the occasional van or passenger car stopped in the breakdown lane, hood up and steam rolling out. We crested the top of the hill at 48 miles per hour - right where we had been on the entire climb. As we hit level ground, Eddie proudly stuck out his chest and began to pick up speed. Soon we were rolling along at a crisp 65 miles an hour as I watched the temperature gauge drop to 200 degrees.

Eddie had passed the first big test.

Barbara and I both shouted, "Hallelujah!" We slid over into the high-speed lane and headed south - south, toward Fancy Gap, *and perhaps Eddie's biggest test yet.*

Within an hour or so, we intersected with Interstate 77 at Wytheville, Virginia and turned south toward the North Carolina border at Mt. Airy (the home of Andy Griffith and the model for the fictional Mayberry). The final approach into North Carolina is an imposing hill called Fancy Gap. From the top, looking eastward toward Mt. Airy and Winston Salem one might think he was on approach to the airport. It is one of the most beautiful vistas in the world as well as an imposing drop off close to 8 miles. The southbound lane has several *"truck escape ramps"* to provide a means of escape for runaway trucks who brakes can't handle the pressure.

For weeks, I had imagined all sorts of fiery, mangled endings to this moment. I was as convinced that Eddie would be difficult to hold back on this decline as I was that he could not make the climb at Christiansburg. For days, I had studied satellite images of the road from top to bottom, marking in my mind where the escape ramps were, just in case. I would lie awake at nights, thinking I could smell the brakes as they caught fire and melted off Eddie's ancient rotors. Now, the moment of one of my greatest fears was just ahead.

I slowed to 55 miles an hour - and then to 45 as I took my foot off the accelerator, letting Eddie coast along, my foot poised over the brake pedal. Again, I shouted to Eddie — and I think to the heavens as well — *"Here we go - take it easy!"*

As we crested the ridge to begin our descent into North Carolina — *or oblivion*, Eddie began to pick up speed. I thought, *"Here we go."* I was now resting my foot on the brake pedal, ready for any feeble attempt to slow Eddie down before he went completely out of control to hurl us into the abyss. I gripped the steering wheel so tight my knuckles hurt, my heart was pounding in my chest. I had endured nightmares about this moment for months, and now it was upon me.

Imagine my surprise when Eddie did not careen out of control. He slowly picked up speed until the speedometer reached 55 miles an hour. And there we stayed - 55 miles an hour for the entire 8 mile descent. Apparently, Eddie has a built-in governor that acts like an engine brake. I never touched the brake pedal during the entire descent down Fancy Gap. As we turned the last corner and saw the road flatten out just ahead as we headed into North Carolina, I looked at Barbara and lied, *"I knew that."*

If your flesh is screaming for you to draw back or take retreat from whatever God has called you to be or to do - *just shout louder.*

4 | Asheboro, North Carolina

(Journal Note): Little change of plans today. We have opted to park Cousin Eddie and watch Hurricane IRMA for a day or so. We are in a hotel in Asheboro, NC and Eddie is safely tucked away in a parking lot next door. We are about a day and a half away from Orlando, and if things go well, we can be there on schedule or if need be, delayed a bit.

We did not have a rigid travel plan when we began our trip, and turns out it is a good thing. We decided on Saturday to stop in Asheboro, NC; park Eddie and get a hotel room for a couple of days. This would afford us the opportunity to have a real hot shower, a more comfortable bed, and a good television by which to monitor IRMA's travel. In addition to being tired, my old ulcer has been acting up the last couple of days causing me considerable discomfort. With some rest, meds, and an abundance of yogurt diet, *I am feeling much better.*

Tomorrow (Monday), we are going to do some early morning maintenance on the RV and head a little further south toward the Walterboro, SC area. The plan is to bed down there for the night to further monitor the progress of the storm. Even though the predictions of Irma's path have changed significantly, we want to make sure that we have a pretty good idea of her timetable before we head any further south. All of our kids will be arriving by air to Orlando on Thursday and Friday as the airlines and Disney are planning on resuming activity by Tuesday of this week. We have reservations there at Fort Wilderness on Wednesday. We will see how this carefully considered plan works out.

Through all of this, it has been an enjoyable time together as we have visited parts of the country we haven't seen in some time. I travel in the south quite a bit with speaking engagements, but Barbara has not been into North Carolina (our home) in almost 20 years.

On our way to breakfast this morning after sleeping in, we walked down the hall toward the front desk. We passed a meeting room and were blessed to the sounds of a tambourine and joyous singing. Apparently, a startup church uses one of the meeting rooms here at the hotel to meet for their worship. It was clearly a very simple worship time. There were tambourines and hand clapping, and adoring voices; no piano, no guitars, or other instruments. We didn't drop in because it was late, and we weren't dressed to drop in on a church service, but it brought back some poignant memories of our childhood.

Our home church, *Lenoir Community Church*, held its first meetings in the ballroom of the Carlheim Hotel in our hometown of Lenoir, North Carolina. Clyde and Louise Triplett, some of the founding members of our church owned the Carlheim and were happy to make the ballroom available to the church in its inception.

I remembered the first service. It was scheduled for a Sunday in early January. We made announcements, passed out flyers, took out newspapers ads to announce the formation of a new, full gospel, Bible preaching church. We were very excited about the new venture. The core group of the new church was The Southernaires Gospel Choir, under the direction of our Pastor (and my mentor, Pastor Bob Parmley), and their parents. We had been a part of a denominational church and in the previous couple of years we had been exposed to the ministry of the Holy Spirit. It was a very powerful, youth led revival that was going on primarily through the choir. Many people had been saved and there were several remarkable healing events. Unfortunately, at that time, the whole *pentecostal* thing was not particularly welcome in this denomination and Pastor Bob was ordered to resign. Bob did not have designs on starting a new church but several members and leaders of the church did and they asked him to continue to serve as their pastor. If memory serves me correctly, the date for the first service was set for January 16, 1966.

Wouldn't you know, we woke up on that Sunday morning in the throes of one of those rare North Carolina snow storms. If you know anything about the south, EVERYTHING shuts down when it snows. Looking out the window in Pastor Parmley's North Main Street home, we peered into an absolute "white out." Pastor was determined that we would not cancel the very first service of the new church.

Sitting in the driveway was the only vehicle we had available to us that day; an old Ford Econoline van - engine in front, rear wheel drive, summer tires; certainly, not a snow storm worthy vehicle. So, we pushed, dragged, and slid the old Ford Van owned by the Southernaires Gospel Choir up the hill along Old North Main Street to the Carlheim Hotel where we began in faith, to set up chairs for the first service of what would become *Lenoir Community Church.*

History will record that the only church in the entire county to hold services that snowy morning was Lenoir Community Church. I was there as we watched people slide up Main Street to the old hotel, many came walking, slogging through the snow while pulling small children on sleds. Through almost a foot of snow they trudged and when we all got there, over 100 people filled up that ballroom. As the worship began, the Spirit of God fell on the place. God's people showed up and found that the Lord was there already, *waiting on them.*

Over the years that followed, Lenoir Community Church became one of the most influential churches in the entire area. In fact, I was privileged to have lunch with the church as they enjoyed the celebration of their 51st year of ministry. Pastor Bob

Parmley served the congregation for over 40 years before passing away at the age of 72 on November 7, 2011 after a brief battle with cancer.

Pastor Bob was not only my pastor; he was my mentor; he was the only father I ever knew. I had the privilege of preaching at his funeral. In attendance at his memorial service were scores of men and women who were impacted and trained by this anointed man. Before the service began, I stood near the front of the church and watched as familiar faces, albeit much older, began to flow into the building. From all over America we traveled to pay homage to the man who brought a unique vision for ministry into our community and into our lives.

I remembered vividly the humiliation, the rumors, the lies that my best friend endured as this new work began; *not from the world, but from the church.* Christian brothers and sisters spread all sorts of vicious rumors, including the most hurtful of all that Bob was a homosexual predator preying on young boys under the guise of ministry. Since I was one of the closest to him, it was alleged that I was his homosexual "boy". One of the sweetest, kindest men I had ever known; a man who pulled me out of a pit that I will not describe here was subjected to the most brutal treatment one can imagine. He never complained. He never struck back. He remained always faithful to the calling that God had put upon his life and spread across this land are men and women who were touched by his life, serving the Kingdom and fulfilling his legacy. *I am one of those men.*

As I stood for those few moments in the hallway outside the meeting room at the Comfort Inn in Asheboro, North Carolina listening to the sweet sounds of worship coming out of that rented room; I was transported back in time more than 50 years to a time of great joy, and in my mind, I could see faces that I have held dear all these years. Clyde and Louise Triplett, Grandpa Smith, Mack Edmisten, Bill and Loretta Hefner, Bill and Lois Lawson, Grace

McGinnis and Dessie Watson, and so many others. I could just about hear that old Hammond organ with Pastor Bob seated at the keyboard and the sounds of saints, many of whom have been promoted to eternity singing,

"We've come this far by faith, leaning on the Lord;
trusting in His Holy Word, He never failed me yet. Oh, Oh, o Oh,
we've come this far by faith."

I was barely 16 then. In just a few months I will celebrate my 69th birthday. Barbara and I still cherish that wonderful heritage, the legacy that was left us in the Southernaires, Lenoir Community Church, and my best friend, Bob Parmley - - and realize that *"we've come this far by faith."*

I did not realize when we fired up Eddie and left Brattleboro for Florida that we would visit not only geographical places, but another time as well. I stood there in the hallway of that hotel and remembered a time when my foundations were poured and the many people who poured them. Barbara and I come from good spiritual stock. Our heritage in Christ is strong. My only hope is that I will leave a generation with a legacy as rich as was left to me.

I continued down the hall toward the front desk and as I turned the corner, the music faded from my hearing and I whispered, *"I love you Bob."*

5 | *St. George, South Carolina*

Hurricane Irma is turning northwest. The latest forecast from the National Weather Service is good news for Florida as she has turned from her potentially devastating track right up the Gulf Coast to a more central landfall and track. Great for the coast of Florida, not so great for Central Florida and people who are heading for -- you got it -- *Disneyworld.*

We are caught up in Irma's tail as she turns to the northwest toward Kentucky, and have decided to sit it out for the night. Radar shows it clearing up later tonight and sunny tomorrow. We are having a great time as Eddie steadily rocks back and forth in the wind and the rain falls against the roof and the sides; sleepy kind of weather. Barb is reading a book and I'm thinking about taking a nap. Great day for a nap. We are under a tornado watch (Again? Didn't we just do this in Pennsylvania earlier last week?) Don't fret over us - we're having a great time. I am with my favorite gal and she. . . .*well, she has a book.*

One additional note: The driving rain has done us a great favor, *kind of,* in that it has exposed all the roof leaks that we *didn't* find last week. Now, when it dries out, I can fix them! *Yea!* In the meantime, the kitchen chorus of pots, pans and bowls is playing our favorite medleys of drip, drip, sploosh, plop, and clang.

The saga never seems to end. We finally got a brief break in the rain and decided to walk over to the Truck Stop terminal and get a bite and stretch our legs. Barbara loves Barbeque sandwiches and I love hot dogs. It so happens that there is a Dairy Queen at the truck stop, famous for both their hot dogs and Barbeque sandwiches. O my, were we in for a big disappointment. First, the place was p-a-c-k-e-d with people. Apparently, we weren't the only ones riding out the storm at this spot. They had no ice in the soda machine and they had no Cole Slaw for my hot dog "all the way." When Barbara got her Pulled Pork Barbeque sandwich it was loaded with pickles. When I say "loaded with pickles" I don't mean that the sandwich had pickles on it. I mean that the pulled pork had been mixed and served with pickles in it; literally, saturated with pickles and pickle juice. Miss Barbara did not enjoy her Barbeque sandwich. Mr. Michael did not enjoy his hot dogs "all the way" and neither of us enjoyed our warm sodas.

And then. . . . . . .

As we walked back from the terminal, I looked across the lot at Cousin Eddie. Something didn't look right. I saw that the cover for the air conditioner was standing straight up in the air, like the hood of an old Chevy pickup. The wind, at some point, had picked it up and there she stood. At the same time, (mind you, we've been here for over two hours) I noticed that I failed to turn off the head and marker lights when we stopped. I thought, *"Great, now water is pouring through the AC unit into the interior and the battery is dead."*

I sloshed my way over to Eddie, unlocked the door and woefully sat down to verify that our battery was completely drained. Imagine my delight when the engine turned right over and there was no water coming into the interior; at least no more water and none through the air conditioner unit that was now completely uncovered. The clips that are supposed to hold the AC cover down were completely unseated and unusable. I devised a quick repair plan which required me to climb onto the roof with a drill and self-tapping screws, lie down on the wet roof and drill holes through the cover to the metal case of the AC to fasten down the cover. At least the rain had stopped and the wind had died down. *Right? Right.*

38

I got into my tool bin and retrieved my cordless drill, a box of bits and a handful of self-taping screws and climbed the ladder up to the roof. Just as I lay down to begin my work, the rain came back. Just as the rain came back, the wind came back. Great sheets of rain driven by huge gusts of wind. It was like trying to thread a needle in the path of a fire hose.

There I was, lying on my side in two inches of water in driving wind and rain, trying to drill holes and tap screws. *End of story?* Cover is safely fastened down, though temporary; I am soaked to the bone, also temporary.

WE'RE HAVING AN ADVENTURE, AND GOD IS STILL GOOD, HE HASN'T MOVED FROM THE THRONE, *AND WE'RE STILL REJOICING.*

Post Script: There is this damnable fly in here that will surely meet its maker; if I can just move fast enough to affect an introduction.

DAY SIX: Walterboro, South Carolina

I entered partial retirement at the end of last year and this past July, Barbara closed her Registered Day Care after more than 30 years. I am still preaching and advocating for the Deaf in Kenya and Barbara is tending her garden and doing some limited child care for families that are close to her, but not enough that she requires registration.

My children have been planning this big Disney Vacation for almost two years. At our age, we had no interest in driving straight to Florida and then back to Vermont just so we could hug Mickey Mouse. So, I had this GREAT IDEA! I bought a 1976 Cruise Air Motor Home. My children immediately dubbed him "Cousin

Eddie", which means nothing to anyone who hasn't seen Chevy Chase and Randy Quaid in *"Christmas Vacation."* While Eddie is old, the engine has relatively few miles on it and I thought, *"What could go wrong?"*

This attitude has been the bane of my entire life. I cannot count the number of times I have asked this question only to have the answer served up in technicolor and surround sound.

Over the course of last winter and spring I have been "refurbing" Eddie - even right up to the last minute when on the night before our departure my good friend Tim Mitchell and I were crawling around under Eddie trying to unfreeze the emergency brake. Undaunted and resplendent with a 4-foot decal emblazoned on the hood - we hooked up our little Volkswagen Jetta on a tow dolly and fired up Cousin Eddie for our "big adventure."

We are now about 6 days into our journey and have endured a tornado in Pennsylvania, which produced several leaks in Eddie's roof due to tree limbs being thrust through it, concluded that Eddie gets FAR WORSE fuel mileage than I ever dreamed (4.8 mpg), we have learned that you must lock down the tow dolly after you load the car on it before you can move, and discovered that Eddie has, as one friend put it, the aerodynamic qualities of a brick.

This afternoon, in St. George, South Carolina we took refuge in a Pilot Truck Stop. The wind was driving the rain so hard it drove water right through one of the side panels and soaked Barb's bed (not mine) with water. The rain also established irrefutable evidence that I had fixed some roof leaks discovered in Pennsylvania and exposed all the leaks I had missed. The wind lifted the AC cover on the roof effectively rendering the air conditioner useless and requiring me, in gale force winds, to climb onto Eddie's roof to reattach it so as not to blow off into the parking lot.

My Facebook page is filled with a barrage of posts ranging from, *"Are you out of your mind,"* to *"Do some more stupid stuff, this is hilarious!"* Apparently, some members of my family in North Carolina got together just to read our updates and ROFL. *By the way, Jeannette Plummer Gantt, I hope you DO wet your pants.*

For those of you who wait with bated breath on the next installment of our adventures, I hope you enjoy them as much as we are. *We're having a ball!*

Barbara and I have spent our lives together in one big adventure. We started out together over 50 years ago as teenagers actively engaged in world changing ministry. I have been preaching the gospel since I was a teenager and for better than 48 years now, Barbara has been right by my side. We've been told more times than I can count, *"You can't do that,"* or *"It can't be done,"* and the frequent, *"for heaven's sake, are you out of your mind?"*

God has allowed me to travel the world and preach and teach in some of the most exotic and remote places you can imagine. I have slept in mud huts, crossed rivers infested with crocodiles, been accosted by bandits, walked among lions. I have stood at the edge of Victoria Falls and strolled through the lush rain forests of West Africa. I have encountered angels and survived tribal warfare in Uganda. I have strolled the ancient cities of Europe and beheld the grandeur of the Alps. I have beheld the stunning shorelines of Australia and Tasmania.

So, sitting here in a parking lot in St. George, South Carolina with our old RV rocking back and forth in the wind, trying to keep as much water as possible from soaking our 1970's "shag" carpet, as we watch in wonder as the winds of Irma push water right through the walls of the RV (on to Barbara's seat); Barb and I are doing what we have always done - *We are living.*

Too many folks our age are not living at all. *They're waiting to die.* My very wise son once said in a sermon, *"The goal in life is not to arrive at death safely."* Oh, how I shout agreement with that sentiment. As I approach my 69th birthday, the ugliest thing of which I can conceive is to die, rotting away in some hospital bed, plugged into machines with tubes and wires. We're all going to die, unless the Lord returns first, and I watch so many people who, instead of maximizing each day God gives them, spend the whole of their lives trying to avoid death. One simply cannot enjoy life while focusing on not dying. Death remains an enemy, but since the death, burial, and resurrection of Christ you can be assured that for those of us who trust in Christ, *Death's bark is a lot worse than his bite.* Many fear desperately the "other side." I don't. Not at all, because I know who waits to greet me on the other side.

Many years ago, I took an old man with me on a trip to Kenya. Ken Lane was old and sick, and many people feared the trip would kill him. Friends urged me not to allow him to go for fear the rigors of the journey would surely be too much for him. My answer, *"What more glorious doorway through which a man of God to enter into eternity than in a moment fully engaged in the work of the Kingdom."* Ken Lane did not die on that trip though it was difficult for him and at times I did think he might. He survived. He did not stop talking about that experience for the more than 15 years he lived after returning home.

On that day when I pass from this life into the next, I truly hope I drop dead in the pulpit preaching the gospel to lost men on their way to hell or, in a remote village at the rim of the Great Rift Valley delivering the Good News to men who've never heard. Lacking that, I hope I am on another great adventure with my best friend and life's partner; giving no quarter to the enemy, not relinquishing a single moment of victory to him, spitting in the

42

devil's eye every day and declaring that he will not steal, not one moment of the life more abundant that Jesus purchased for me.

How will you spend your days?

6 | St. Augustine, Florida

The continuing saga of Eddie, the little bucket of bolts that was pretty sure he could.

Last night was spent in the parking lot of the Pilot Truck Stop in St. George, South Carolina. It was a lot like sleeping on the edge of a wind tunnel as the remnants of IRMA swept through South Carolina and Georgia. Not only was the wind rocking the RV from side to side like one of our ill begotten men's fishing trips with (the only thing missing was Zach Kendall puking over the side and Ken Labbee bragging about how many fish he caught), it was literally driving the rain right through the seams in Eddie's side panels and up and under - and then down through the roof vents. It was a lot like driving through a carwash with the top down. Great fun! Barb and I laughed like a couple of kids - *well me more than her because it was her bunk that got wet.*

The morning broke with a beautiful blue sky and a warm sun. The wind was gone, the rain was gone, Eddie hadn't used any oil, the coolant levels were up, and I thought, *"What could go wrong?"*

Well, actually, a few things could go wrong.

First, as I turned up the street to merge back onto southbound I-95 I realized that *EVERYBODY* that had evacuated Florida in front of IRMA was now returning home. Some of them were in a big hurry. Some of them were very rude. And clearly, some of them flunked driving school. It looked a lot like they had opened the doors to the asylum, given everyone a set of car keys and said, "You are free to go!" Have your ever driven bumper cars with a bunch of circus clowns. I have - *today.*

44

Then there was the issue of gas; as in none – anywhere. If you have been following us on this little journey you know that Eddie likes his gas in copious gulps. We have 70 gallons of tank and he can drain it faster than Dale Jr. can clean off a Mt. Dew.

We filled up in Walterboro, South Carolina and headed out for Florida. Since there was a lot of traffic, it was a slow, leisurely drive south. The traffic, though congested, moved with a steady clip for a few miles and then we would approach an exit. Apparently, exit ramps cause great consternation to some folks because every time we got within a mile of an exit (about every 10 to 15 miles) the whole procession would grind to a halt as some cars tried to get off while on the other side cars were trying to get on and those in the flow of traffic were clearly bumfuzzled by the entire process.

But, we pressed on, with Eddie happily guzzling on gas as we proceeded. It was somewhere around of Savannah that we realized that the National Guard and State Troopers (in the south, we don't have State Police - we have TROOPERS and perish the day you don't understand the difference), had sealed off EVERY EXIT and as a hapless result, EVERY GAS STATION! Further and further we drove, and every exit was sealed off by ARMED men with very large GUNS.

It did not take long for me to come to understand that it wouldn't have mattered if they had allowed us to exit - there was no gas, and if there was gas, there was no electricity to run the pumps. We were not going to buy fuel in South Georgia.

Eddie either did not comprehend our plight or Eddie did not care about our plight, as he made absolutely no effort to repent of his gas gluttony. His gas greed continued unabated.

FINALLY, GLORIOUSLY, THANKFULLY we crossed
St. Mary's River and entered the beautiful state of Florida. As we
approached the first exit we saw no armed men blocking our
access to gas.

It was at this point that we, along with every south bound
traveler on the eastern seaboard exited the highway and headed for
the one gas station at the end of the ramp. I don't know how many
of you ever saw the movie, "It's a Mad, Mad, Mad World" with
Jonathan Winters and Spencer Tracy, but the carnage at this fuel
stop was comparable.

Automobiles, motorcycles, trucks, RV's and guys walking
with big red gas cans converged, unaware that two pieces of matter
cannot simultaneously occupy the same space, or if you prefer –
pump. It looked like Bumper Cars on steroids or maybe a
Demolition Derby had spilled over from the fairground into the
streets. It was a street fight in the barrio, a brawl in the Bronx, a
revolution in the Basques.

So many cars and trucks were pushing into the station,
starving for fuel and completely bereft of mercy or patience. They
were lined up on both sides of the highway, cutting off thru traffic
in either direction. I gritted my teeth, waiting for the gunfire to
erupt.

Realizing the situation, I spun around, got back on the
interstate and implored Eddie to consider our plight and cooperate
a bit on the fuel consumption. He burped and farted as we went up
the ramp and ignored me completely.

As we drove further and further south, we realized that
there were no gas stations pumping gas. They were locked up
tighter than a Scotsman at Tax Time. As we passed by one exit,
just north of St. Augustine, we looked off the bridge and saw a
small truck stop that was pumping gas. Please note; just as we
passed the exit. We drove south for a while and decided that we

would stop at a Walmart and park for the night. We chose Walmart because ALL WALMART FRANCHISES WELCOME RV'S FOR OVER- NIGHT PARKING. *They are well known for their southern hospitality.*

Well, as it turns out, not *all* of them. Not the WALMART in Palm Coast, Florida. As we pulled off the highway, low on fuel and lower on enthusiasm we turned into the Walmart parking lot at Palm Coast, Florida only to be greeted by the most unwelcoming and unfriendly signage:

NO OVERNIGHT PARKING.
VIOLATORS WILL BE TOWED
NO TRUCK PARKING. NO RV PARKING.
NO SLEEPING IN CARS.

You know, to suffer rejections is a bitter pill; ever or anywhere, by anyone. But, can you imagine how humiliating it is to be rejected ....by WALMART? I mean *seriously?* Turned away by Walmart?

Running low on fuel, we made the decision to go back north to the Flying J Truck Stop at St. Augustine and at least fill up to satisfy Eddie's insatiable thirst and ease our minds. We arrived a few minutes later to utter chaos; bumper cars on steroids. Even through the madness we prevailed and were FINALLY able to fill Eddie up with more than enough gas to finish our journey to Orlando tomorrow. Taking note of the growing chaos in the parking area at the Flying J Truck Stop in St. Augustine we made the decision to again head south to a state highway rest area and visitor center that boasted all night security. *Surely we can enjoy a quiet, restful night there.*

In the middle of all of this, my oldest son called. You know it is going to be an interesting call when it begins with the words, "I need you to talk me out of something."

You see, we weren't the only ones having issues. Bryan, and his family of seven were supposed to fly into Orlando on Sunday night (the one that was already over). However, due to the impending and unpredictable arrival of Irma, his flight was cancelled.

It was also cancelled on Monday.
It was also cancelled on Tuesday.

And Wednesday, *and Thursday.*

They could get on a flight out of Boston late on Friday which would get them into Orlando early on Saturday morning. The problem with this scenario was that by Saturday an entire week of their vacation would be gone. Bryan was unable to change plans much on the other end because of work schedules for he and Rebecca. He had been working non-stop since Monday morning, trying to get another flight to Florida that didn't involve staying in Vermont until their vacation was over.

"O.K. What do I need to talk you out of?"

"I have found a flight from Boston to Atlanta on Wednesday, but I can't get a flight from Atlanta. I think I'm going to fly to Atlanta, rent a van and drive to Orlando. It's only six hours."

"Well son, that's not entirely a crazy idea. Mostly, but not entirely. It's not a terrible drive from Atlanta to Orlando, but I can foresee one potential problem."

"What's that?"

"You will remember that there were hundreds of thousands of people who fled the hurricane and they are going to be coming back home at the same time as you. I predict you will be driving in extremely heavy, slow moving traffic and that gasoline is going to be another whole problem. Other than that – great plan!"

"Would you do it?"

"Well of course I would, but you have to consider that I am sitting over on the other side of the state in a 41-year old RV facing the same kind of traffic as you and needing gas a whole more than you will. So, I may not be the best judge of what is a good idea."

"O.K. then, we're going to do it. See you in Florida on Thursday morning."

It took Bryan and his family two hours to fly to Atlanta. It took Bryan and his family 18 hours to drive from Atlanta to Orlando. I relate this story only to establish proof that I'm not the only one in the family who is not real bright.

Here is a notation from my journal: We are now bed down at a Rest Area on I-95. The ambiance is delightful. I mean who doesn't enjoy the sound of trucks rumbling by every 2.1 seconds, the roar of engine brakes, and the genteel conversation of weary travelers at the top of their lungs. *What more could a fellow want?*

Barb is reading and I am reflecting and what I'm thinking is this: *"in all these things we are more than conquerors through him who loved us. For I am sure that neither death nor life, nor angels nor rulers, nor things present nor things to come, nor powers, nor height nor depth, nor anything else in all creation, will be able to separate us from the love of God in Christ Jesus our Lord."* (Romans 8:37-39 ESV)

Life is not always easy. Life is not always fair. Life doesn't always go the way we want it to and things are not always the way we think they should be - *but God is always faithful.* His mercies are always sure, and His grace is always rich.

We get despondent when we focus on the injustices of life. We get discouraged when God doesn't follow our neatly laid out plans and because of it we miss out on the joys of life that are ours if we will only open our eyes and appreciate them. We spend too much time belly aching and not enough time reveling in the fact that we are alive, we are loved, and we have the opportunity another day to live our lives in such a way as to cause men to glorify our Heavenly Father.

It was prognosticated by several wise and knowledgeable folks that Eddie wouldn't make it to the Massachusetts border, let alone all the way to Florida; and yet here we sit, 1200+ miles later and a scant 112 miles from our destination. *(My tongue is sticking out at all of you doubters and naysayers)* We are resting under the umbrella of the Palmetto tree and listening to the music of the state bird of Florida (the mosquito), we are warm (really, really warm), it's not raining, the wind is not howling, our kids are on their way to meet us for a great family vacation; *and we've got gas.*

What more could a guy ask for?

7 | FORT WILDERNESS

We woke up today somewhere north of Daytona Beach after spending the night in a rest area on Interstate 95 in Florida. So many people were returning to their homes after evacuating from the path of IRMA, the place was more than full. It was brimming. During the night, cars would pull through and finding not even a spot on the grass, they just went on their way. Amazingly, Barbara and I both slept well, anticipating our arrival at Disney and then, over the next few days the rest of the family will arrive.

It was a beautiful Florida day. The sun was shining, not a cloud in the sky and you could just tell it was going to be *hot*. We were a scant 112 miles from Fort Wilderness, we had a full tank of gas, Eddie ran flawlessly yesterday without so much as a hiccup. We both had a nice bowl of cereal and milk, packed away all the loose stuff, buckled up our seat belts and prepared for a nice ride down to Disney.

Around 8:00 a.m. it was all systems go. I checked the oil and fluid levels. Tugged on the straps on the tow dolly to make sure the car was safely secured, checked the hitch on said dolly and made sure all the hatches were closed, put up the step up, closed the door and sat down in the Captain's chair, looked at Barb and said, "Let's go Babe!" I turned the key that wakes Eddie up aaaannnnnddd. . . . . . *nothing.*

Not a whine, not a groan, not a grunt or belch; no effort whatsoever. The batteries (both of them) were dead; D-E-A-D; deceased, expired. Apparently, at some time during the night Eddie had suffered a heart attack and died. Poor Eddie. I must admit that all the smoldering frustration I had been concealing under a jovial, *"we're on an adventure - we're having fun!"* facade almost leaked out.

Just as the thinly disguised rage that had been lurking in the hidden places of my heart began to crawl out from under the covers and expose me for what I really am, a very tall man with a exquisite handlebar mustache stepped in front of the van, looked straight through the windshield and pointed a camera at my face, "Cousin Eddie! What a great name for this wonderful old piece of antiquity! I'll bet you guys are having a great time. Please, let me take your picture; my kids are not going to believe this!"

I quickly grabbed all the ugliness that was about to rear its ugly head and stuffed it back down inside wherever I'd been hiding it, smiled and said, "Sure, I know your boys will get a great laugh out of it." As I posed, I displayed my very best phony smile and said cheerily, "Say - you don't happen to have a battery charger with you, do you?"

He laughed and said, "Sure do. Isn't that the great thing about these old rigs. The engine runs great but you need a rear-view camera to keep track of all the parts falling off."

If he only knew how true his words were. He pulled out his charger as we rigged up a series of extension cords across the median to his rig and put the charger on the battery. It turns out that during all the bouncing and jouncing during the day before, a wire from the positive side had broken and created a short in the electrical system. Easy fix and within 45 minutes we had enough juice transferred from one old rig to another to revive old Eddie and he roared to life. I could almost hear a EMT's voice shout, "CLEAR!" as I turned the key and electrical impulses flowed into that old heart and much to both our delight, Eddie roared to life.

As we waited for Eddie CPR to take effect we chatted and I learned that Bob and his wife (and parakeet) had evacuated their home in the Florida Keys and were on their way back, in hopes they still had a home. Suddenly, our little battery issue took a whole new level of irrelevance. I had sat up very late the night before, watching thousands and thousands of cars, perhaps tens of thousands of cars; aware that somewhere on the other side of the state, my son and his family were driving in the same thing. Millions of people struggling to get home, *many of them not sure that they still had a home.*

My little minion of rage that had tried to surface was sent back to his hiding spot for another day as I prayed for Bob and told him we would be thinking about them as they headed home. I am assuming Bob and his wife and parakeet are home now, and with all my heart, I hope they found more than a pile of rubble when they arrived.

So, with Eddie displaying his most throaty rumble, I again took my place in the Captain's chair, pulled the gear lever to D, and pulled out into traffic on a beautiful, sun filled day, feeling pretty smug that we had faced that challenge handily and with a new charge of electrons flowing into Eddie's powerful engine, we were off to Fort Wilderness.

The drive from Daytona down to Orlando was remarkably uneventful. There was some pretty heavy traffic once we got to the big "O". Actually, the traffic was horrendous, with a great deal of construction going on, but I am an experienced driver having once worked as a coast to coast semi operator and we negotiated the massive traffic jams in the city pretty handily. I was proud of myself. I was especially delighted when the lovely lady who lives inside our GPS announced, "In one-half mile exit to the right toward Epcot and Walt Disney World."

I said to Barbara, "I think it is not imprudent to make an announcement: WE MADE IT! Eddie made it all the way from Vermont to Disney." Turns out that it was in fact an imprudent statement, for within seconds of making that proud announcement, I heard the ramps on the tow dolly scrape on the road. I thought, "That's not right." I looked in side mirror only to see one of the tires on the tow dolly had gone flat, and by flat, I mean flat: deceased, depleted, empty of the stuff that makes it go bounce, and there was no place to pull over. So, I pulled into the main gate at Fort Wilderness to a security guard charging out of the gate house waving her arms frantically and screaming,

"Ya'll know you got a flat tire? And IT'S ON FAR!"

The tire wasn't actually "on far," it was smoking pretty badly though. I said to my little rage demon that had been trying all day to escape, "Go back to your corner, I got this."

I leaned over to the window and said, "Yes, I am aware but we'll just pull over here into the parking lot and I'll take care of it within the next day or so."

"Oh no - you can't stay here. Fort Wilderness is CLOSED because of the hurricane. They've arranged for you to stay in one of the resorts until we are able to open back up again. You can't stay here and you can't leave that 'thing' here."

In that instant, my mind's eye could see Clark Griswold and his family running (in slow motion) across the parking lot at WALLY WORLD, finally there after a long and arduous journey across the country only to be confronted by John Candy, "Sorry, we're closed for repairs." (I was trying furiously to remember where I had hidden my BB pistol.)

Through the fog of my frustration I heard the lady say, "They're going to put you up at Pop Century until we reopen. You'll have to drive over there." The ensuing conversation went something like this:

ME (In my most conciliatory voice): "Ma'am, I can't drive it anywhere. I have a completely ruined tire. It needs to be fixed."

HER: (In a completely clueless tone of voice): "I'm sorry, you have to take it out of here, you can't leave it here. They won't let you."

ME: (In a slightly less conciliatory voice): "Honey, I can't take it out of here until I can effect repairs. I need a new tire."

HER: (She really said this): "Well, you'll have to get someone to come tow it."

ME: (Completely unwilling to any longer be conciliatory): "I'M TOWING IT NOW. Do you think a TOW TRUCK is going to have any better luck at this than I am?"

What we finally agreed on is that I could pull into the parking lot, remove the Volkswagen from the tow dolly; jack up said tow dolly, remove the wheel, put it in the back of the Volkswagen, and find someone who would sell and mount a new tire for me. (Remember how I reported that the night before I had been REJECTED by Walmart? Well, now I must confess that I have been SAVED by Walmart.)

We drove the almost 16 miles to Clermont, Florida to a Walmart Super Center where I could purchase and have mounted a new tire. We drove back to the completely closed Fort Wilderness, re-installed the tire, put all the tools away, put the Volkswagen back on the tow dolly and drove to the Pop Century Resort whereupon I entered said facility only to remember that one of the most vaunted features of any Disney Adventure is STANDING IN LINE!

I could hardly believe my eyes at the line which stretched from the Concierge Desk through at least a mile of those neatly arranged barrier tapes, filled with parents who had long ago given up any hope of controlling their children, being attended to by what must be the most patient receptionists one could ever hope to meet. They stood and smiled with interminable patience while they answered every conceivable mundane question known to man while not once – not even once – showing the least hint of impatience or frustration. I, on the other hand. . . . . . HATE STANDING IN LINE.

You know, we once hosted a guest speaker who joined us all the way from Texas for a series of meetings. He spoke each evening, but during the day I made sure that he could take in as much beauty of the Vermont countryside as possible. I took the entire week and drove him to many of our most popular spots. He seemed very happy to have me as his chauffer for the week.

On the very last day of the week in a sermon about character he said, "Someone once asked me how best to discern a man's true character."

He smiled, looked directly at me and said, "Oh, I usually have him drive me around for a week or so. *That can be pretty revealing about a man's character.*"

Another way is to watch him while he is forced to wait in a long, slow moving line. Barb sat down while I held sway in the que, awaiting some attention from one of those famous "Disney" smiles. Outwardly, I was the image of suave, collected patience, while on the inside, I was a seething cauldron of molten impatience, convinced that the receptionists had colluded against me, hoping to bring me to the brink of insanity before. . . .

"Welcome to Disney! How may I help you today?"

"What!!!?? Oh, uh, sure – Hello, I'm Mr. Coolness who has been waiting patiently while you so skillfully have attended to the needs of all those wonderful people who got here before I did."

We have been checked into, at no additional charge, a beautifully air conditioned room (Did I mention how hot it is here this week?) for the entire duration of our stay at Walt Disney World. While Eddie swelters in the Florida heat in a remote corner of the Pop Century Resort, we are cool as cucumbers beneath a giant five story cell phone at this lovely resort.

There is more - so much more - that filled up this day, but that is for another story. Let me close today's log by saying this:

We *didn't* have a flat at 65 miles an hour on the expressway, but on an access road where we completely out of danger, and at a greatly reduced speed.

Instead of sweltering in the Florida heat, which we more than willing to do as a part of our great adventure, we are safely and comfortably ensconced in a beautiful and comfortable room without incurring any additional expense.

We were able to drive 32 miles (round trip) to a service center that had ONE trailer tire that fit our tow dolly.

Likely, when we return to Vermont in a few weeks we will find our beautiful home on Western Avenue awaiting our arrival; unlike the tens of thousands of Floridians who drove home today to a pile of rubble that used to be home; unlike my new friend, Bob, who graciously took part of his morning to help a stranger in need who drove his own RV home with a heavy heart not knowing whether his home is there or not.

I'm tired. Bone tired. I am fully convinced that I will never undertake such an arduous journey with Cousin Eddie again. It's just too tiring for a couple of old folks like Barb and I. We're having a ball, but thinking that while this is great fun - it's almost too much fun. Eddie may get to visit Cape Cod or up to our family camp in Central Vermont, or even down to Amish Country - *but no more border to border journeys.*

I'm sitting here in the dark recording just some of the events of this amazing day listening to the sound of my wife's steady breathing, picking up message dings on my phone alerting me to arrival times of my children and grandchildren and thinking, *"What a great day! What a great adventure! What a great God I serve!"*

My rage monster is again sulking in his room, no doubt plotting his next attempt at escape and my heart is heavy; but not for me - for Bob and his wife and their parakeet, and so many like them who drove home today only to find that home had been washed away in the fury of a storm.

Good night Bob. I pray you can sleep well.

8 | A PHONE CALL AT MIDNIGHT

What a relief on Wednesday to park Eddie and check into the POP CENTURY DISNEY RESORT. Because of storm damage, Fort Wilderness is closed and we have been rebooked into one of the Disney resorts for the entire 9 days of our stay here. This of course mean air conditioning, nice hot showers and bus service to all the various venues. It turns out that God chose to bless us beyond what we asked or expected. *He is good like that.*

With God's power working in us, he can do much, much more than anything we can ask or think of. (Ephesians 3:20 ESV)

We had a nice, restful evening last night. We went out to dinner, went for a long walk, and talked about how nice it would be that our two younger boys, Andrew and Timothy would be arriving today and then our daughter and two of our grandchildren along with Robyn, our oldest daughter arriving soon after. It won't be long until the ENTIRE Gantt/Stires clan would be together for a great family time together.

Sometimes, when the phone rings you know -- *you just know* -- that it's not good news. At exactly 4:35 a.m. this morning (Thursday) my phone rang. My heart sank as I picked up the phone and answered dreading the news I was about to receive. It was Timothy. He and his wife Heather and daughter, Cadence were in route to Bradley Field in Hartford, CT for a 6:00 a.m. flight to Orlando. 30 minutes from the airport, they received a text message informing them that their flight had been cancelled.

He was continuing to the airport to see what the matter was and if they could be booked on a later flight. They had nothing for them, except a notice that they would refund their ticket price within five business days. They were willing to book them on a flight on Saturday. Since Tim has just started a new job, his time is limited to the days booked, so Saturday was not an option. It was go today or go home.

To have the entire family here with Tim, Heather and Cady at home simply did not seem to be an acceptable option; so we went to work, and from 4:30 a.m. until almost 8:00 a.m. Tim was trying every airline in Hartford to find an alternative flight while I was on the computer trying to find something to get them here.

I finally booked them on a flight at 7:59 p.m. from TF Green Airport in Providence, Rhode Island. Heather's poor mom then drove them from Hartford, CT to Providence, RI; after which she had to drive back home to get to work; leaving Tim, Heather, and a 3-year-old stranded at the airport **for the next 10 hours.** EXCEPT. . . . . (you just knew it wasn't going to be THAT easy). *Just two hours before their departure the status on their flight changed to "delayed."* When Tim checked in he was told their plane had been grounded in Denver for maintenance issues and would be significantly delayed. More waiting for them; more worry for me. I felt so bad for them. When they finally get to bed, they will have been trying to get to Florida for more than 24 hours. They could have driven Eddie here in a shorter less time!

The good news is that they are finally in the air and according to my flight tracker they are 36,000 feet above Winston Salem, North Carolina, flying at 453 knots and scheduled to arrive here at 1:15 a.m. (And yes, I always track my children when they are flying so that I know exactly where they are always.) Andrew, Hannah, Eliana, Alexander and Nessah are on another airplane scheduled to arrive here just after midnight. You just knew it couldn't be so simple for us as to have them get on an airplane and soar right down here. *There just HAD to be some drama.*

There is a sub-plot to this story. I believe and have always taught my children that "the steps of the righteous are ordered by the

Lord." (Psalm 37:23) Sometimes, in the middle of our frustrations and irritations, even our inopportunity we forget things. We forget that the Lord is ordering our steps, and who knows what dangers lay ahead that we never see, nor do we even know about that the God who loves His righteous ones, simply walks us around.

God was with Joseph when he was dragged off to Egypt, and God had a plan. Joseph could say to his brothers *"what you meant for evil, the Lord meant for good."* It might have seemed to Joseph to be a terrible inconvenience, even tragedy, to be sold into slavery in Egypt, but it was God who was behind it all. When his brothers arrived, starving, to get food Joseph told them, *"God sent me before you."* God sent Joseph to Egypt to prepare the way for the deliverance of his family.

It was the same for Daniel, Shadrach, Meshach, Abednego; it was the same for Esther, Ezekiel, and Zechariah. God ordered their various steps for their ultimate benefit and His ultimate glory. We were created for the express purpose of bearing His reflection to a dying world that they might see Him and be drawn to Him.

When God changes your plans; even when it puts you in great stress; remember that the *"chief end of man is to glorify God and to enjoy Him forever."* Instead of praying, *"Get me out of this mess!"* Ask God to show you why He brought you through this and to this place. You will enjoy wonderful peace and great blessings.

Before I close today's entry, please bear with me for one great little story. Barbara and I spent the day at ANIMAL KINGDOM with our oldest son, Bryan and his family. We had a great, fun-filled time, the details of which I won't bore you with other than the fact that my son said to me with a wicked grin on his face, "When was the last time you rode on a REAL roller coaster?"

I reminded him that I took him on his first roller coaster ride and that I *love* roller coasters. He said, "Good - come with me."

At that precise moment we turned a corner and came face to face with an incredible replica of Mt. Everest and in the distance, I could hear people screaming in terror as if they were being ground into hamburger meat. It was at that precise instant I saw a coaster train shoot out of the side of that mountain on an almost vertical descent, at which point I muttered under my breath, "Me and my big mouth. " I was too terrified to ask the big question,

"WHAT COULD GO WRONG?" I didn't ask because there were clearly a multitude of things that could go wrong.

My kids were so anxious for me to ride this thing that they even got me a "fast pass" so I wouldn't have to wait in line, because knowing how I hate long lines, were sure I would utilize the obvious excuse. Nope, marched straight into the loading area and stepped right into a cart with my beautiful granddaughter Emmalee and as we pulled down the safety bar she looked at me and said, *"You're gonna love this!"* There were so many things about that ride that my children simply failed warn me about. So, up Mt. Everest we went and then down Mt. Everest we came and I survived - TWICE! Yes, just to show what a manly guy I am I stupidly said, *"Sure, I'll go again."*

As we walked back to rejoin the rest of the family my granddaughter, Maddisen remarked, "I think I left my heart back there at Mt. Everest."

I thought to myself, "I am pretty sure I left a bowel movement back there at Mt. Everest."

However, I must hasten to the end of today's story. We escaped the incredible heat by going to one of the shows, "Festival of the Lion King." It was an utterly delightful 45 minutes with incredible costumes, music, acrobats, animation; superb production value. The house was packed and the audience was thrilled. Since I have a background in theater, I was beyond impressed.

At the finale, various cast members came into the audience to select children to march in the closing number, the "Circle of Life." The faces of the children who were chosen were truly luminescent as they danced out onto the floor, playing the little instruments provided them by the cast members. Seated just to our right was a beautiful little blond, maybe 4 years old, significantly disabled and confined to a special wheelchair.

She showed no disappointment or dismay when children around here were chosen and she was not. It was clear that she was accustomed to being left on the sidelines when others were chosen for special things.

Just before the finale began, a beautifully costumed man, dressed as a leopard came out of the chorus line and knelt down in front of this precious child and with a huge, welcoming smile said, "Would you honor me by being my partner for the Grand Finale?"

Tears ran down my face as her face lit up as if she had just been presented the Crown Jewels of the Queen. He joyously pushed her around and around the stage as she beamed and waved and beamed and waved and beamed and waved. . . . *and he smiled as if he were escorting a real princess.*

I took note of the fact that this handsome and talented black man made sure that this beautiful little blond white girl didn't get left out; that she had the opportunity to be a princess along with all of her peers and not be left sitting on the sidelines like a useless cripple. I am so weary of the phony narrative a racism that is being waved like a flag of hatred, designed to further divide us from one another. There was no racism at Disney today. There was no racial superiority at Disney today. There was no manufactured racial divide. There was a man. Not a black man - a man; a man filled with compassion, dripping with personal charm and charisma, a man of enormous talent. A man who spotted a beautiful princess who just needed a prince to guide her chariot.

Blessings my friends.

9 | REFLECTIONS

I moved from North Carolina to the northeast in 1967. Two years later, I went back to North Carolina, put a ring on Barbara's finger and brought her back north with me. We spent two years together in Western Massachusetts while I finished college and in the fall of 1971, I agreed to pastor a small church in southern Vermont.

We moved to the Brattleboro area in February of 1972 and Bryan was born in August of that same year. What ensued from that point were many years of ministry during which we have built wonderful and endearing friendships, engaged in years of rich ministry; often despite us more than because of us, and suffered some moments of very regrettable failure.

More than once I have been the victim of my own ego, the engineer of my own downfall, and the instrument of great pain and disappointment in others. I have at times impeded the progress of the Kingdom rather than to advance it and have brought shame upon the Master instead of bringing Him glory. Though I understand I am as prone to human frailty as any, and more so than a lot; and even though I am completely conversant with the Biblical reality that God forgives us of our sins when we have a repentant heart; I still look back with an ache that wishes I had been a better man, a better father, a wiser, more spiritually mature pastor so that so many people I love might have suffered fewer wounds and less disappointment.

Over the last few days I have been reminded that God is fully aware of my weaknesses and despite them can use me. He is able to overpower my frailty and design the perfect instrument to prick my overblown ego and bring me again and again to a place of humility. I can also see more clearly this week how richly God has blessed me, in spite of my failures, in spite of my sometimes-poor judgments. There is much fruit growing up behind me for which I must give God the glory.

During the last week or so Barbara and I have made our way to Florida enjoying some hilarious moments along the way and enduring some difficult times with a level of grace that can only come from God. In the ensuing days, our children have all, finally, gathered with us along with some precious friends.

When Barbara and I first moved to Vermont there were just the two of us. I was so young and so arrogant I had no idea what I didn't know. There are now 23 of us and we are all gathered in Orlando enjoying a great time together. Five children and 12 grandchildren and not one of them unaccounted for in the Kingdom.

My heart is full tonight as I think of them: Bryan (the eldest) and wife Becca, Robyn and her husband Wayne, Andrew and his wife Hannah Marie, Timothy and his wife Heather, and Abigail. Those are the children God has blessed us to birth and raise. Of course, there is also Matthew Keith who awaits us in heaven.

It is with great joy, I list for you our grandchildren as well: Gabriel, Hannah, Emmalee, Maddisen, and the foster (prayerfully soon to be adopted) child I call *Goober*. There is also Grace, Noah, and Riley, Eliana, Alexander, Nessah Louise, and Cadence Israel.

The words of the Psalmist weigh heavily upon my heart tonight:

Except the Lord build the house, they labor in vain that build it: except the Lord keep the city, the watchman waketh but in vain. It is vain for you to rise up early, to sit up late, to eat the bread of sorrows: for so he giveth his beloved sleep.

*Lo, children are an heritage of the Lord: and the fruit of
the womb is his reward. As arrows are in the hand of a
mighty man; so are the children of his youth. Happy is the
man that has his quiver full of them: they shall not be
ashamed, but they shall speak with the enemies in the
gate.* (Psalm 127 KJV)

I am also reminded tonight of the words of one of my
missionary heroes, Jim Elliot, written to his parents in defense of
his decision to go to the mission field:

*"Remember how the Psalmist described
children? He said that they were as a heritage from the
Lord, and that every man should be happy who had his
quiver full of them. And what is a quiver full of but
arrows? And what are arrows for but to shoot? So, with
the strong arms of prayer, draw the bowstring back and let
the arrows fly -- all of them straight at the Enemy's hosts.
"Give of thy sons to bear the message glorious, Give of thy
wealth to speed them on their way, Pour out thy soul for
them in prayer victorious, And all thou spendest Jesus will
repay."*

With each post I have logged for this journey I have been
encouraged by the enthusiastic response from so many friends. I
have noted that most of my friends are delighted at the funny
things that we have encountered along the way and I apologize if
you were looking for some humor in today's post. I hope you
realize that Eddie is parked for the week and most of the humor is
somehow woven into his existence.

Today, I'm tired, a little lame, and still recovering from the
last, "Hey Dad, come ride this. You're gonna love it!" I don't

know where the mad scientists are that design some of these things are locked up, but they need to throw away the key and forget about parole. These guys are demented sadists who delight in the torture of the elderly. They clearly sent letters to my kids saying, "Get your Papa on this thing - it will get even for every time he's tricked you into pulling his finger."

They seem to delight in watching the "terror" on my face. They seem to think I'm afraid I'm going to die. The truth is, on some of these rides, I'm more afraid I'm going to live and have to ride another one. I've rumbled off Mt. Everest, screamed through Big Thunder Mountain, and rocketed through Space Mountain. I have descended into the mines of the 7 Dwarfs, and battled the Empire in a rocket ship - and much to the delight of my grandchildren, I'm still alive to be abused another day. I think they don't realize that I took their Fathers on their first roller coaster rides. I suggested such to one of my grandkids the other day only to be scoffed at and told "that can't be true - they didn't even HAVE roller coasters way back then."

My quiver is full and I am a happy man. I have weapons to fire at the enemy and they are sharp and eager. I am watching my boys as they have become great dads and my girls are godly women and mothers who are more like their mother than they will ever know. I have especially enjoyed watching Bryan and Gabriel interact this week as they have maneuvered this mass of humanity from one event to the next. They have carefully thought through each activity for the past several days so that we all end up at the same place at the same time and they are more alike than either of them realizes.

My heart swelled today as the guide for our African Safari at the Animal Kingdom declared as we took over his entire safari truck that, "this family was the most unique and entertaining family he had ever taken through the park."

You know what? He's right, and I am so blessed that my God is bigger than my failures, stronger than my weaknesses, and that His grace is greater than my sin and I declare for all this night, His blessings are richly disproportionate to what I deserve.

10 | TACOS SUPREME

It's 3:15 a.m. on Tuesday morning, and Tim just served up an order of *Tacos Supreme*. Apparently, he was not aware that he had placed the order. It just sort of just showed up, unannounced, and altogether unwelcome. It sure made his trip to the Magic Kingdom "magical." Food can give a certain added sense of adventure to a ride on Thunder Mountain and a new spin on the Tea Cups. Certainly, thinking about Tim as he flies home on Wednesday. He may actually have a *special seat* on that flight.

It's 4:30 a.m. on Wednesday morning and I'm sitting outside under a giant figure of Roger Rabbit balancing on a can of turpentine and a huge yellow "Walkman," drinking a cold can of Cheerwine. I'm thinking about heading out for a plate of Liver Mush and Grits in a while and getting hungrier by the minute.

I've just come from seeing Tim, Heather, and Cadence off to the airport for their flight home. I've just learned something about the little one: She is real grouch when you wake her up before she is ready. I will be praying for their little family as they fly back home today. It seems like just such a short time we were fighting to get everybody here and now, over the next few days we all start toward home. The kids will all be flying while Barb and I, well - *we definitely won't be flying* - we will be pointing Cousin Eddie northward (kinda) and moving out of here on Friday morning.

You know, it's hard work having fun with 25 people ranging in age from 5 months to 816 months; from 66 cm tall to 199 cm tall, weighing from 2.7 kg to 143 kg; not to mention getting them to wear the same exact shirt and to show up at the exact same event at the exact same time. It's tough to arrange work schedules, travel schedules, housing arrangements and event schedules to work together. (Not to mention one certain little guy's first haircut.) Bryan has worked (in partnership with Gabe and Abigail) for over two years to organize and direct this little family outing to coincide with our retirement. I am positive he would have had a great deal more fun and relaxation if he would have left us at home and traveled with just his family. However, he has been the oil that has greased this machine. The only thing missing is a red umbrella to carry at the head of the line so we can all find him.

I'm sure he's had a great time planning this adventure and I'm pretty sure he will NEVER invite us all to come to Florida with him again. However, in the meantime, he's done a great job and we are all grateful for his hard work and commitment to our family. He is the firstborn, every bit the elder brother; and not at all like that elder brother in Luke 15 who despised the younger.

Instead, Bryan seems to have taken his greatest joy this week in making sure that his siblings and his parents have an enjoyable time. He has pushed strollers with little ones while their parents have gone off to enjoy an exciting ride or show, and asked his mother at least a thousand times if she is "doing all right."

It has truly been a typical Gantt family extravaganza; loud, boisterous, everybody talking at the same time, engaging everyone we meet and pulling them into the maelstrom that we call family; and hard to tell which kids belong to which adults as everyone has pitched in to make it a great week. It has been so much fun watching this bunch invade a room or restaurant and immediately, like a band of traveling comedians, "work" the room and then blowing out the door like a caravan of jesters in red shirts leaving unsuspecting travelers wondering, *"What just happened?"* They are truly a force to be reckoned with. Have I ever told you how much I love my kids?

It breaks my heart to see families broken and shattered; fighting over an inheritance, frozen in a moment by some perceived "wrong;" pushing their own blood out of their lives because of offenses, real or perceived and living in unforgiveness and bitterness; bitterness that slowly chokes the life out of the one who gave us life or, those to whom we have given life, or, those with whom we share life. When we do this, we not only break our own hearts, *we break the heart of God.* Our families are the first and greatest gift God Has given us apart from Jesus, our Savior; and other than Jesus, they are our first line of defense against the attacks of the enemy.

Satan, from the beginning has worked to drive wedges in the family. He wants to destroy marriages, alienate siblings, harden the hearts of children toward their parents, transforming families into war zones, rather than safe havens for us all. I don't hold our family up as a perfect model. We have our spats, our conflicts, our troubles just like everyone else. However, there is a model that Barbara and I hold up for our children to see and it is the model of the scriptures.

God has given us vivid pictures of marriage and family and if we will faithfully use its template, we and our children will enjoy God's blessings and the spiritual prosperity the Bible promises. In *Deuteronomy 6* and in *Psalm 78*, among others, God tells us that in the context of family, and through the power of Jesus' blood that we destroy the work of the devil and strengthen one another against his attacks. When we allow ourselves to be alienated from our family we expose them to the attacks of the enemy and make them, and ourselves, more vulnerable to his devices.

Barbara and I are constantly engaged in warfare for our children and grandchildren. We will allow nothing to alienate us, we reject anything that might divide us, we rebuke in fervent prayer any effort of the enemy to bring destruction into their lives, marriages, or children. We teach our children the principles of Scriptures *"that it might go well with them in the land."* [Deuteronomy 6]. Even this trip is not solely about "fun". It is about fortifying our family against the evil plans of the enemy against them.

Barbara and I had a nice day yesterday. Andrew took all the guys out for breakfast (except for Tim who wasn't feeling well and Gabe who had plans otherwise) to a Shoney's Buffet Breakfast. Then Barb and I took the day off from having fun to rest. We're finding more and more that us old folks must put ourselves in time out with a bit more regularity than we used to. Fun is still fun, but you must take it in smaller bursts with long naps in between. She went shopping with one of our girls and her family and I drove the 40 miles or so up to Sanford, Florida to visit with my good and longtime friends, Steve and Sue Dunklee.

Like other folks I know, Steve doesn't seem to really know how to deal with this whole "retirement" thing so, while he's retired he has served as an interim Pastor in a couple of places and accepted a position at Ethos360 (formerly New Tribes Missions) as a chaplain for their retirement facility for NTM missionaries. Even though both he and Sue have had some significant health issues over the past few years, they soldier on in the service of King and Kingdom. For now, they live in the middle of some 70 acres of missionary housing and a thousand stories of unrecorded history regaling the majesty of the King.

In just a short time there, I met an aging missionary pushing along a walker who was born with Cerebral Palsy, writing with her left hand because her right side was so limited, told that she would never live, never walk; that she would be dependent for her whole life sharing with a huge smile telling me that she spent 50 years climbing up and down the hills of Papua New Guinea sharing the gospel of Jesus Christ. After recently falling and breaking her hip, she was told she would never walk again. She laughed as she stood up and pushed her little walker down the hall. Oh, to have the time to just hear all the stories that live in that beautiful little compound.

We ended our day at Andrew and Hannah's with Eliana, Alexander and Nessah so their mom and Dad could have a nice evening out together. The kids swam in the pool, Nessah rolled around on the floor and I answered Alex's "why" questions at least 1,345 times.

The sun is coming up, another day has begun and I get to spend it with the people I love more than life itself. I leave you with this urgent appeal: If there are broken places in your family, if there are wounds that are festering, if there is bitterness which is taking root or long ago planted - do not delay, for both you and those from whom you are alienated are in peril of the enemy's devices and sin is crouching at your door.

11 | COCOA BEACH AND BEYOND

We left Orlando and Disney on Friday morning of this week and pointed Eddie due east toward the coast. Barb remarked that she did not come all the way to Florida to not visit the seashore. So, it was off to Cocoa Beach and the Sonshine RV park, a lovely little park about 12 miles from the beach.

I mentioned to Barbara that I have been to Florida several times in the past few years, but this is the first time in more than thirty years that I was in Florida and not working. I have visited the state numerous times over the years representing the Kenya Development Fund and the Immanuel Christian School for the Deaf, speaking at conferences and churches, but not since my middle son, Andrew was around five months old have I been in Florida for non-working reasons. It was then that it occurred to me: I haven't been pretty much anywhere in the past thirty-five years when I wasn't working. I'm ashamed to make that little revelation, but the truth is that I have spent a great deal of my life working, to the exclusion of pretty much everything else.

Which brings me back to Cocoa Beach. In the late fifties and early sixties, I lived in Orlando (this was of course, pre-Disney]. I spent a lot of time as a kid at Cocoa Beach which lies just forty miles or so east of Orlando. My mom worked at the Cherry Plaza Hotel in Orlando as a waitress and I started my first business in 1960; lawn care. At the ripe old age of 11, a friend and I borrowed his dad's lawn mower until we could make enough money to buy our own and I went to work. I have pretty much been working ever since.

I was devastated when my mom told me that we were moving back to North Carolina to run a restaurant for my grandfather in Lenoir, North Carolina. I loved living in Florida and I was sick of moving. Little did I know at the time that God was moving me toward my destiny, for it was in Lenoir that I was introduced to Christ, called to the ministry, and met the girl who would eventually become my wife.

I have quote to my children repeatedly from the Word of God, *"The steps of the righteous are ordered by the Lord."* Though the pathway we walk may be difficult and will often take turns we never expected and we may go with our heels dug in, kicking and screaming; *God has a plan.*

My grandfather was an angry and abusive man who treated my mother terribly and the last thing I wanted to do was to leave a place where I was happy and move in with THAT man. I didn't want to be around him and I surely didn't want my mother to endure his abuse any further. Yet, I realized much later that God was ordering my steps all through my life and while I had to endure a lot of things that were unpleasant and even cruel at times; God had a plan, and he eventually brought me to the place where all the pieces to my essentially aimless life came together.

Who knows what might have become of me had my grandfather not bought that stupid restaurant, which by the way, he quickly bailed on and left my mom holding the bag; stranded and unable to move, in Lenoir, North Carolina. As it turns out, that's where all the pieces to the puzzle of my life were laying, waiting for my arrival.

I'm wondering, what pieces are you not seeing in your life and where might they be laying, just waiting for you to arrive. The steps of the righteous are ordered by the Lord, *often even before they are righteous.*

I know some of are waiting with bated breath to hear the latest news on the continuing escapades of Cousin Eddie. I am happy to report that during our stay in Orlando and even over to Cocoa Beach, Eddie was well behaved. If you don't count the fact that he refused to start on Friday morning at Disney, he caused no problems at all.

We drove over to the coast and spent the better part of three days relaxing, going to the beach, and resting up from the frantic days roaming around the various parks that are Disney World.

This morning, we awakened early, packed up Eddie, disconnecting him from all the various tubes, hoses and wires that make him our home away from home. We loaded the VW onto the tow dolly and headed north on Interstate 95. As we left the RV park we stopped at a little gas station to pick up some ice for the coolers, gas up Eddie, and put some air in a tire that was looking a little soft. After that, we were off.

I must say that even though we were bucking a strong headwind all day (for those of you who have seen Eddie's photo, you know he is not particularly aerodynamic], Eddie ran beautifully up the sunny Florida coast. As we were winding our way through the city of Jacksonville a little Prius came roaring up beside us, honking like crazy. I'm kinda used to that now, because a LOT of people honk and laugh when they see Eddie. But this guy as a little too persistent as he honked and honked and as he pulled up alongside, honking and GIVING ME THE FINGER!

I have had people point, and giggle, and outright howl when they look at Eddie and realize that we've driven him all the way from Vermont. I have had people ask to have their picture made with us to show their kids. I have even had people BLOW their horn with obvious irritation because Eddie doesn't move as fast as their little Camrys or Geos but this is the FIRST TIME SOMEONE HAS SHOT ME A BIRD! I mean the very idea. *Eddie is ugly, but come on.*

77

Suddenly, I realized the man wasn't giving me the finger, but he was frantically pointing up; up, like toward the sky and then it began to dawn on me that this kind gentleman was not mocking me; he was WARNING ME. Something was wrong and he was concerned. Unfortunately, I was right in the middle of Jacksonville on Interstate 95 and it was not convenient or safe to pull over - but then I remembered:

You may remember the account of us sitting in the waning winds of IRMA an nearly losing the cover on Eddie's air conditioner. That night, I climbed up in the driving rain and howling wind and effected some pretty nifty repairs, even if I do say so myself. They sustained that air conditioner cover perfectly.

That is, until today, in the middle of Jacksonville, Florida.

When I could find a reasonably safe spot to pull over, I jumped out of the RV to see what the man was so frantic about, and there it was: The AC cover had come completely off. It was lying flat on its back, held there by only a single ⅜ inch piece of copper tubing. If that thing had flown off and hit someone's car it could have been tragic.

So, if anyone reports seeing a crazy man, in the middle of Jacksonville, Florida on top of an antique RV wailing away at a piece of copper tubing trying to dislodge the AC cover so it didn't kill somebody - - **that would be me.**

The offending cover was tossed into the RV until later when I could strap it to the back between the ladder and the spare tire and we were off, Eddie's hat now safely rescued and him purring like a kitten toward Georgia.

At some point along the way we stopped to switch gas tanks. This involves stopping alongside the highway, getting out of the RV and reaching up to a manual valve to change tanks. I won't bore you with a long explanation as these events took place before the Great Adventure began. Back inside, signal to the left, merge into traffic, bring Eddie up to speed and we SHOULD have been roaring up the road. Instead, Eddie began to cough and choke and gag and lose power, much to the irritation of the many, many travelers who were speeding along at seventy miles an hour while Eddie could barely maintain fifty miles per hour.

Now, there was more honking, and hooting, and finger shooting; using now a different finger. Those fingers were meant for me and I am sure they weren't warning me about something getting ready to fly off the roof. We did this for fifty miles, all the way back to Walterboro, South Carolina where we now sit, parked on the backside of a Wal-Mart Parking lot.

My initial diagnosis is fuel filter. The replacement part has been procured and will be installed at first light. If my efforts do not result in a smooth-running engine, our next plan involves loading Eddie on to the tow dolly and pulling him home with the Volkswagen Jetta. In the meantime – it's hot, it's late, I'm tired - and you have all the images you need to laugh yourself to sleep tonight or, if you've already gone to bed, to giggle your way through breakfast.

Good night, love to all

12 | A STAR IS BORN

In yesterday's post, I remarked that Eddie had suffered a pretty severe indigestion attack as we came up the road from Florida. Somewhere in Georgia we switched gas tanks (which you do a lot when you travel with Cousin Eddie). We had filled the auxiliary tank up as we left Cocoa Beach and it would appear there was something in the gas that simply did not suit Eddie's delicate, aging system. So, for more than 100 miles we choked and gagged our way northward, unable to exceed 55 miles per hour and managing to irritate almost every other driver around us.

We limped our way into the Super Wal-Mart in Walterboro, South Carolina; our pre-planned destination. I had already decided that the problem was fuel based and probably due to some bad gas that had no doubt clogged the fuel filters. I called my trusted mechanic friend, Mark Stockwell, who listened intently *(between snickers and giggles)* as I described our latest issue, hoping he could confirm my diagnosis.

I must add here that were it not for the able assistance and wise counsel of both *Mark Stockwell* and *Tim Mitchell*, I would probably have never gotten out of the driveway with Eddie, let alone all the way to Florida and back. I called on both numerous times when I got stuck with problems I couldn't seem to solve. They were great. Although, I do seem to remember Tim asking to NEVER see Eddie in his driveway again.

Mark agreed with my conclusion and recommended that I get to the nearest auto parts store and secure two new inline filters. I googled auto parts and found there were three stores within two miles of our location. I unloaded the VW from the tow dolly and while Barb pondered our evening meal, I ran off to get fuel filters. By the time I got back, it was dark and I was tired - and supper was waiting. Eddie's repairs would have to wait until morning light.

Cue Morning Light: I got up early this morning, got out my tools and rolled underneath the RV and set about replacing the fuel filters. I ALWAYS seem to forget that those things have GAS in them and when you pull the lines off you can get a face full of gas; which I did – twice. Obviously since the first one had gas in it, the second ought to be empty - *RIGHT?* Finishing my task, I crawled out from under the RV, put away my tools and smelling very much like a Texaco station stepped to the door whereupon my wife with a big smile, handed me the *lighter* and said, "Would you be a dear and light the gas stove so I can cook breakfast?"

Sleeping with one eye open tonight folks - *on my guard for sure.*

Breakfast done, we pulled into Murphy's USA gas station and topped off both tanks. I held my breath as we turned onto the northbound ramp and accelerated to the highway. Although, with this rig that's gobbling up gas at the rate of just UNDER 5 miles to the gallon, ACCELERATE is such poor terminology. Lumbered would be a more clinical appraisal of what Eddie actually does when you push on the gas pedal. It is almost like when you tell your kid to go to his room. He starts toward the room, but the motivation to get there is quite low, and the progress is slow and filled with grumbling all the way down the hall.

So, as Eddie "lumbered" up the ramp - I held my breath, but as we merged into the northbound lane at the blistering speed of 32 miles per hour, Eddie was purring like a kitten, or groaning like a hippo, or something - but he WASN'T stalling out and by the time we got to the next exit we were up to a nice 65 miles per hour and we were on our way!

Since the coast of North Carolina is expecting heavy rains and winds this week courtesy of yet ANOTHER tropical storm, we headed west from Charleston toward Columbia, South Carolina and from there northward on I-77 toward Charlotte, NC. I stopped along the way and made reservations for a RV site at Ebenezer Park in Rock Hill, South Carolina. It is a beautiful park situated along the shores of Lake Wylie and maintained my York County in South Carolina. I have a cousin who lives in Rock Hill and an Uncle who lives in Gastonia, about 20 miles away. My cousin is dropping by in the morning for a quick visit. Tonight, Barb and I enjoyed a nice meal at Cracker Barrel before driving down to the Crowder's Mountain area to visit with Uncle Jim. He is the only remaining sibling of my mother and at 90 years old is still very sharp. He has been struggling with Parkinson's Disease for several years, but has a great spirit about him. *I love the man dearly.*

However, I must tell you that today, along the shores of Lake Wylie in South Carolina a STAR WAS BORN. We checked in to Ebenezer Park, found our spot and began to set up for the night which includes hoses and wires to provide water and sewer and electricity. We even hooked up the water heater and boy does it feel good to wash your face and hands in good, clear heated water - courtesy of the little water heater in Eddie's frame.

However, the setup was a bit surreal as slowly, people began to emerge from the various trailers, fifth wheels, massive motor homes and look our way with looks of awe and wonder. It was as if a great celebrity had arrived on the scene, or Godzilla had just arisen out of the waters of Lake. Little electric golf carts with little old men began to drive by, circle the field, and drive by again, pointing and gesturing with rapt wonder at the sight of Eddie proudly occupying his space in all his regality and splendor.

I couldn't figure out if they were caught up in Eddie's ancient beauty or if they were wondering if the Clampetts had just

82

arrived from Beverly Hills. There was pointing and gesturing and waves and polite smiles as the little parade of golf carts continued past our space. One lady stopped her pickup truck, got out and walked across the grass to where I was rolling up some excess wiring, put her hands on her hips and just looked at Cousin Eddie for a long, breathless moment before asking, "Just how old IS that thing?"

I explained to her that Eddie is our 41-year-old marvel, with a Dodge engine and the heart of a champion. "And you drove that RV ALL THE WAY FROM VERMONT?"

"No," I explained, "All the way from Vermont to Florida - and now we are headed back to Vermont."

She looked again, slowly walking around the site, and finally said, "Are ya running from the law?" She grinned and shook my hand she said, "Well, I gotta say one thing - Ya got some mustard in yah." As she walked away, I heard her mutter, "Un-stinkin-believable!"

Later, I was taking a little nap when I heard Barbara whisper, "Michael, there are some people out in front of the RV - a whole bunch of them and they are taking pictures." I sat up and looked out through the windshield where sure enough, there was a small gaggle of folks taking turns snapping photos of themselves in front of Eddie, right where the hood is monogrammed with the words, *"Cousin Eddie."*

I stepped outside and said to one guy, "I guess I'm going to have to start charging a fee for these photo ops."

He smiled at me and said, "Too late buddy, these things are already on the internet. CHRISTMAS VACATION is my family's favorite movie and we've been sending these photos to our entire family all over the southeast."

Just as they were walking away, one of the older gentlemen stopped and turned and took one more look before asking, "Just how old IS that thing?"

So, on the shores of Lake Wylie in Rock Hill, South Carolina - a star is born and his name is "Cousin Eddie."

I am amazed that people were so intrigued by this old antique as they were at seeing him lumber down the road and pull into a hook up site. Eddie is an anomaly amid the huge, luxury motor homes that inhabit these sites today. He is not long and sleek and powerful with sliding walls, and heated saunas in the back, with built in satellite television systems. He is old but rugged, slow but sure; a reminder of a day gone by back *when "they really built them,"* as one fellow remarked today. He sure looks different we noted as we drove out of the park as Eddie sat, dwarfed by huge mansions on wheels and slick and speedy tiny homes hooked to the back of a diesel pickup.

He looks different, because he IS different.

If you are a Christ follower into today's culture, you are an anomaly. You are different, off-beat from the rhythm of a modern, self-centered culture. You hark back to another time, another culture, another set of values; values largely forgotten or abandoned in our world. People may laugh or mock, unable to comprehend what makes you tick. You may hear the occasional, **"Un-stinkin-believable!"** The world may laugh, point fingers, even snap a "picture" for their friends so they can have a good laugh too.

Please do not be put off by the fact that you are different from your friends or your neighbors.

YOU ARE SUPPOSED TO BE DIFFERENT!

Jesus has pulled you out of a dying world and made you a citizen of His Kingdom. He has, through His blood, cleaned all the crap off you and clothed you with robes of His righteousness. This world literally has nothing to offer you, because everything that has meaning you already hold in your hand. You have the spark of life in you in shadow of the pall of death. You are alive and you are NEVER GOING TO DIE!

"Un-stinkin-believable!"

13 | HOME ALONE

Barbara and I returned home this week after almost a month on the road in our first extended vacation in several years. What a great time we had. Some of our more sadistic "friends" seem to take delight in some of the struggles along the way with our antique motor home, lovingly dubbed "Cousin Eddie." It seems like every day we saw person after person log on to our Facebook account pleading for an account of the latest adventure with Eddie. By adventure, I mean, "what roadside disaster had we encountered?" What fell off in the middle of the highway? It seems like everybody was drooling over the next account of what appeared to be the latest episode which often looked more like an episode of "keystone cops" than it did a vacation.

Sadly, on Wednesday September 27 just north of Roanoke, Virginia Eddie suffered a near fatal "aneurism." As we were approaching mile marker 146, near Troutville, Virginia I noticed that the temperature gauge was rising rapidly. I nursed Eddie along until we could get to the exit at mile marker 150 as I knew this to be an exit with multiple truck stops and presumably, truck repair centers. We did exit at the Troutville exit and found a parking lot where we could stop to examine Eddie to see what the matter might be.

I was deeply disappointed as I knelt in the dusty parking lot to find that Eddie was "bleeding" severely from the water pump - hence my diagnosis of an aneurism. I knew instantly that Eddie would not be making the trip home to Vermont with us. We would be traveling without him the rest of the way. I seriously considered putting him out of his misery (more correctly - out of

MY misery), but (A) didn't have the heart after he had worked so hard for the past month and (B) *didn't have my revolver with me.*

While I was in fact disturbed about Eddie's condition, the truth might be closer to the surface if I confessed that I was most worried about the stockpiles of Cheerwine, Liver Mush, and Duke's Mayonnaise we were carrying back to Vermont. I feared that we wouldn't be able to carry our clothes, personal items, AND the precious treasure trove we had stowed safely away inside Eddie. Barbara, as compassionate as ever, informed me that we would be bringing the cooler with ice and liver mush, but he Cheerwine and Mayonnaise would have to stay with Eddie. I wept. [If you don't know what these precious commodities are, or don't like any of them, feel free to read on. If you do, please pause for a moment of silence and reflection.]

As we sat in the dusty parking lot behind McDonalds and beside the Motel 6 with the temperature hovering around 95 degrees I called AAA to see if they could get a tow truck to carry Eddie to what I supposed might be his final resting place and whether they could recommend a competent geriatric mechanic in the area who would work on the ailing and aging Eddie without requiring that I leave Barbara as a hostage to guarantee my return. After a disappointing encounter with AAA in Florida regarding a flat tire on the tow dolly, I was suspicious that they were prepared to do anything except accept my next year's subscription check. However, this time, AAA did us right.

First, they found a wrecker that could haul the old boy to a garage, depending of course, on whether we could find someone who would tackle the task of stemming the tide of coolant that was gushing out of Eddie's superheated engine. They assured us that a wrecker would be dispatched within the next two hours (I don't think they realized how hot it was sitting in Eddie with no air

87

moving and a rapidly rising inside temperature. But they are southerners and quite frankly, I don't think they cared.)

They also recommended David Wood at *Botetourt Truck and Trailer Repair* as a potential miracle worker to consider the task of bringing Eddie to life again. The lady at AAA recommended that I call him since we had nothing to do for the next two hours *(which turned into nearly three)* until the tow truck arrived. I called him. The conversation went something like this:

"Hey this is David."

"Oh, hello David, how are you?"

"Fit as a fiddle but not nearly as pretty."

"I am calling on the recommendation of AAA who suggested that you might be the man to help me out."

"I'd love to help you out, which way did you come in?"

(I already like this guy)

"Well, I came in from Rock Hill, South Carolina this morning on my way back to Vermont."

"VERmont - ain't that in Canada?"

"Well, almost - but anyway, my Motor Home broke down - I'm pretty sure it's the water pump. Eddie overheated pretty quickly and there is a flow of coolant dripping down the center of the engine."

"O.K. Yer water pump broke - but who is Eddie? You lost me there. Is he traveling with you?"

"Er, no - it's a long story but Eddie IS the Motor Home"

"Is this a joke? Are you funnin me?"

"No sir - there is absolutely nothing funny about this. My kids named it Cousin Eddie, kind of after a movie......."

"Wait a minit - I jus need to axe you a question?"

"What's that?"

"Was Wally World closed when you got there?" (laughter through the whole shop - because of course now, we're on speaker phone.)

"Well, now that you mention it...in a manner of speaking - yes." (more laughter on the other end.)

"Well what kind of RV is Cousin Eddie?

"1976 Cruise Air on a Dodge frame with a 440-cubic inch Chrysler engine."

"1976!!!! You don't need a mechanic - you need an elephant gun!"

"Yeah, I thought about that, but I had to leave my guns in Vermont. But, to the point at hand - would you be willing to let me tow it out there and see if you can fix it."

"Oh, I kin fix it; just don't know if you kin afford it!"

"Yeah, that's what I thought."

"Caint (that's a real word where I come from*) git to it this week, but maybe next week I could take a look; bring her on out here."*

"Great - I see by my GPS that you are only 4.5 miles from here."

"Yeah boy, but we are a little off the beaten path, just foller yer GPS and bringeron!"

Around 4 p.m. the wrecker showed up and the young man got out, put his hands on his hips, and stared - he just stared. After a while he looked at me and asked, "How old IS that thing?" I shared with him that I get asked that a lot.

He hooked Eddie up, and off we went on a 4.5-mile tour of the mountains of Virginia. We had taken the VW off the tow dolly and were following behind Eddie on the Tow Truck. As we lumbered down Rte. 11 with Eddie wallowing on the back of that wrecker like a beached whale I kept getting whiffs of burning rubber. I thought, "Boy, I hope that's not Eddie," as I had visions of the body of that whale rubbing the tread off the rear tires.

Shortly, Barbara sniffed a couple of times and said, "Is that us?" I thought for a minute and said "Kinda." By now, you could see the dark rubberized smoke boiling out from the back of Eddie and the smell was getting stronger and stronger. I had ideas of rushing up and stopping the tow truck before we burned up a thousand dollars' worth of tire when I remembered that the previous owner had installed two small wheels on the rear bumper so that when you pulled across a hump or ditch, Eddie's bumper wouldn't drag but would ride up on those little rubber wheels. So, when the tow truck raised Eddie's front it lowered Eddie's back.

Let me just say - we're going to have to replace those little rubber wheels when we get a chance.

Finally, we came to Roy Road, a little gravel pathway through the long leaf pines and soon we arrived at the Botetourt Truck and Trailer Repair Shop. David Wood met us with a big grin and a warm handshake as the tow driver unhooked Eddie from the wrecker so I could park him out of the way.

I shared with David that I had to return in just a few days on a trip to North Carolina for some ministry and if all went well, I would pick Eddie up on my return trip. I gave him my card in case he needed to contact me with any bad news (fully expecting I would hear from him within a few hours), and Barbara and I hit the road in the little red Volkswagen for home.

Of course, the ENTIRE northbound lane of Interstate 81 was under construction and so by 10 p.m. we had made it to Chambersburg, PA where we bed down for the night to finish our trip the next day.

This is getting long so I need to fast forward to the last couple of days, because as it has been with this entire adventure with Eddie, when you least expect it - God shows up.

I was expected in Western North Carolina on Saturday and I had two stops I wanted to make on my way south. The first stop was at John and Sheri Parkers home in Red Lion, PA. I sent them a message early in the week asking if I could visit and perhaps spend the night. Always generous hosts, they were delighted to invite me into their home. John and I have been friends for the better part of 45 years going back to when I first came to Vermont. I love John and Sheri very deeply and it was good to see them. As I was preparing for my trip I received a sad message from Sheri, "Dad passed away at 1:00 A.M. Please still come. We'd love to see you. Anything you want special to eat?"

I left Brattleboro on Thursday morning and drove down through the Poconos and eventually arrived at the Parker house in the afternoon. We enjoyed a great dinner, went out for ice cream, shared stories, laughed til we cried, and on top of it, I got to see the Patriot's game on Thursday Night Football. I awakened this morning to the smell of bacon, eggs and home fries and we enjoyed breakfast together. Just before I left Sheri shared with me how special it was that I could visit on this day. She said, "You slept in my Dad's room last night. He was my Father and you are my spiritual Father." That was very special.

I drove from the Parker's to Troutville, Virginia. I stopped for lunch in Steele's Tavern at one of my favorite restaurants, about 50 minutes from the Botetourt Truck and Trailer Repair shop. While I was eating lunch, my phone rang and of all people it was David Wood who said, *"You're all set and your RV is ready to go."* I told him that I was about an hour away and as soon as I finished lunch I'd head toward him.

All the way to Troutville I was thinking about all the fun Barbara and I had enjoyed with Eddie during the month of September. I was also thinking - "This is going to be one BIG BILL." You see, to get to Eddie's water pump, you just about have to pull the whole front of the RV off, remove the radiator so you can get to the engine. I had no idea what the water pump itself would cost, but I was sure that at $80-$100 an hour labor, it was going to be pricey. Besides, I have Vermont plates on the RV, so I was completely at the mercy of this David Wood guy who had to have taken one look at that thing and started perusing Caribbean Cruise folders.

About 2:30 P.M. I pulled into the Botetourt Truck and Trailer Repair. As I walked past Eddie who didn't look at all impressed that I had come back for him, I whispered, "Get used to the south buddy, cuz if this bill is what I think it's going to be, you might be getting melted down and turned into a moonshine still."

David was just finishing up an inspection and when he was done, we exchanged greetings and I explained to him that I was headed to North Carolina and not inclined to take Eddie with me - but that at the end of the week or first of next week I would be back to pick him up. Then I said, "Now, for the million (not literally, I hoped) question: How much is this going to cost me?"

"How much you got?" (sly smile).

"Not a lot, on me, but I can get to a bank and get more."

"Well, let me get the bill and see exactly how much this is going to set you back."

He returned shortly with an invoice in his hand. I gritted my teeth, bracing myself and thinking, "Darn you Eddie - we were almost home!" Through the pain of anticipated financial agony, I barely heard David say, "That'll be $289.99"

I said, "What?"

"I don't know how ya'll count in VERmont (emphasis on the VER), but let me hep you out," as he ran his slender, grease stained finger under the numbers, reading them off to me slowly: "That's two hundred and eighty-nine dollars and ninety-nine cents."

An old hymn came to mind: "Floods of joy filled my soul as the sea billows roll. . . "

The word of God clearly says, "And my God will supply every need of yours according to his riches in glory in Christ Jesus." (Philippians 4:19 ESV)

Sometimes He does that by giving us the money we need. At other times, he arranges for your break down to happen just 4.5 miles from an honest, capable man who will not take advantage of your disadvantage and who will not take note that your license plate that says you are a long way from home and completely at his mercy. God takes care of us in a myriad of wonderful and creative ways, but he always takes care of us.

Of all the places that Eddie's water pump could have given out. Of all the garages in that area (that's why I stopped at this particular exit), God impressed me to call a guy who works off the beaten path on an old dirt road in the hills of Virginia to fix Eddie.

Remember that the Word of God says, "Do not forget to show hospitality to strangers, for by so doing some people have shown hospitality to angels without knowing it." Hebrews 13:2.

All along our paths, God has strategically placed *certain* people in *certain* places who act as *His agents* on *our behalf.* He has prepared circumstances well ahead of time where, if we are faithful, we can be blessed and be a blessing all at the same time.

The *"steps of the righteous are ordered by the Lord,"* is one of my favorite Biblical truths. I forget it sometimes and whine and complain and fret, but then the Lord is faithful to send me to the Botetourt Truck & Trailer Repair and David Wood, just to remind me of his goodness and mercy; and that His eyes run to and fro throughout the earth, seeking a man to whom He might show Himself strong.

14 | BRINGING EDDIE HOME

I left Eddie in the able care of David Wood at Botetourt Truck and Trailer Repair in Troutville, Virginia while I made my way back south to the Carolinas. It seemed odd being on the road without Barbara. We had hardly been out of earshot of one another for almost a month. After many years of my traveling far afield while Barbara managed the household and cared for our growing family, it was a real joy to travel with her for an extended period of time. We enjoyed our trip immensely and I was a bit sad to see our little adventure ending. It was also odd driving our little Volkswagen Jetta quietly down the highway instead of the wallowing and roaring of Eddie. Traveling with Eddie is a lot like straddling a large Roman Candle and lighting the fuse. The fun comes in waiting to see what happens next.

As we had greeted folks in church last week we were warmed by the welcome home we received. Big smiles, great hugs, warm handshakes and a sense of well-being. Eddie had become such a large part of the conversation over the past few weeks that it was at times like we were in the receiving line at a wake; folks offering their condolences, genuinely sad that the old boy hadn't made it home with us. They were happy to hear that I hadn't abandoned him in some redneck junk yard, but would be bringing him home with me in a couple of weeks. The fellows that helped me most in preparing for the trip greeted me with a mixture of admiration and disbelief that we had actually made it THAT far. I think there had been a general consensus that Eddie would never be seen in these parts again.

Now, I was guiding the Jetta through the hills of Virginia on my way to North Carolina for a week of ministry. I was also looking forward to a visit with my aging Uncle, James Gantt; the only living sibling to my Mom. I was happy that I would be spending a few days with him. Jim is 90 and struggling to cope with Parkinson's Disease. It is proving these days to be a difficult battle.

While in North Carolina I was blessed to contact a lot of friends that I had not seen in sometime. I was absolutely amazed at the number of people who had followed our journeys over the previous month. It seemed like everywhere I went, I met folks who had been with us every step of the way from Vermont to Florida and back again. I still a bit struck by the whole thing. I don't know how many times I was introduced as "this is the guy………you know the guy with Eddie…..we've been following him on Facebook."

A man I barely know wrote to me, "I hope I get to meet Eddie face to face someday." (Face to face – I am wondering, "You DO know that Eddie is an RV right?")

A service technician is coming to my house tomorrow to do an installation. I received a note from his wife tonight saying, "My husband just looked at his schedule and realized he is doing an installation for your tomorrow. He is so excited that he is going to get to see Eddie."

It is like Forrest Gump, who decided to go for a run. All along his way, people joined him until there was a huge crowd running with him. We decided, however ill advised, to drive a 41-year-old antique to Florida and post a record of our trip on social media. Without realizing it, more and more people joined our journey along the way and from one end of America to the other our band of travelers grew and somehow, enjoyed our vacation with us.

Eddie is not beautiful. This is not a streamlined powerhouse, a showcase of modern camping technology. He is actually a bit ugly; a red and white box with wheels. The roof leaks, the engine heater doesn't work, the air conditioner is strapped to the back bumper, and everything rattles while you're driving down the highway. He gets less than 4.5 miles per gallon, there is trim held on with duct tape, half of the dash gauges don't work and the ones that do are not dependable. While in 1976 Eddie might have been top drawer, today he is antiquated, outdated, a relic of a bygone era of cheap gas and a pioneer spirit.

When Eddie was built, Barbara and I were just beginning our ministry. We were young, creative, and adventurous -- *ready to take on the world.* We had no clue as to what we were getting into, and I was often guided as much by my own ego and arrogance as I was by the Spirit of God. I hadn't realized it, but as I close in on my 69th birthday, I have been feeling a lot like Eddie; antiquated, outdated, a relic of a bygone era. I am watching as a new crop of leaders arise in the church; smart, gifted, anointed, and filled with zeal and energy. Without realizing it, I had begun to step back into the shadows, feeling that my day was done and it was time to get out of the way.

Don't get me wrong. I am not jealous. I am not bitter. I am excited to see God raising up a new generation of strong, gifted leaders in the church. My own sons and daughters are among them. I am glad. I rejoice in it as I see God raising up new warriors for the battle. And yet..............

And yet, I must confess now that there has been a growing sense of sadness in me that I have been unable, or unwilling, to articulate. I have been so intensely involved in the battle for so many years that to come to a place where I must (*and I must*) give way for a new wave of leaders and cheer them on; I find it comes with an odd mixture of laughter and tears; a stirring of sadness and joy.

I think Eddie somehow represented for me a renewed spirit of adventure that had been somehow misplaced in my life; pushed aside by the familiar, the regular, the safe. For some reason, I was no longer pushing the boundaries; no longer testing the edges. I believe also that the reason our journey created such interest outside our family is that it represented that same spirit of adventure for others; a spirit that seems to have been lost in this time and space. I stood in that man's yard looking at that old beat up RV sitting there looking more like he should be in a junk yard but longing for the open road, one more time.

I thought, "Why not? Why not one more time do something stupid...........and fun!"

As we would drive down the highway, Eddie's old engine rumbling along; newer, cleaner, smoother, more powerful motor homes would roar past, nearly blowing us off the road before disappearing over the rise in front of us. Yet, in day's end, old Eddie would slide into a spot in the middle of those same pristine motor palaces and as I lay down at night I would think, "Yeah, you got here first, but we all got here."

Of course, at that exact moment, I would hear the telltale 'clunk' of something else falling onto the ground and I would think, "Now what!?" As those powerful diesel engines, would fire up in the morning, the electric slides would pull in, horns would toot as they pulled away, I would be on my back on the underside, patching Eddie together for another day's run and I would think, "See you tonight."

Eddie did not finish first, *but he did finish faithfully.*

Eddie was not the best, *but he was the best he could be.*

He was not the most beautiful, but He bears the marks of battle with honor, *knowing that they are but the medals of years of faithful service.*

God does not ask you and me to finish first. *He does desire that we finish faithfully.*

He does not require us to be the best, *but He does ask that we give our best.*

God does not look upon the wounds and scars of our battles with disgust or pity, but with joy *because they mark those wounds testify that though wounded we did not quit, we did not faint.*

"And let us not become weary in well doing, for in due season we shall reap, if we faint not." Galatians 6:9

Upon completing my responsibilities in the Carolinas, I headed back north to Troutville to collect Eddie. On Monday morning, October 16, I pulled the Volkswagen onto the tow dolly and fired Eddie up for our trip home. Sliding up the ramp on Interstate 81, I pointed Eddie toward West Virginia and home. By nightfall we were sitting in a Walmart parking lot in Hamburg, Pennsylvania; about 30 miles from Allentown. I grabbed a sandwich from Subway, called Barbara to let her know I was in for the night, and started to settle in for the evening because I wanted to get a good early start in the morning. Then, it started to get cold. I mean, let's face it I have been living in the tropics for better than a month, and they don't do "fall" in the south like we do in the northeast.

I was lying on the bunk, in a sweater and jeans, wrapped up in a blanket, trying to stay warm when I heard a fan start to run. I was not plugged into an electrical source and I was not running the engine and I thought, "What in the world is that?" I supposed it was coming from the big, shiny motor home parked next to me. But no, that sound was coming from inside. I got up and began to follow the sound when I realized that it was the fan from the furnace -- Eddie's furnace. Now, Eddie's water heater is gas or electric. Eddie's fridge is designed to operate on gas or electric. I THOUGHT the furnace was gas only, and I had turned the gas off - and yet, the temperature had gotten low enough that the thermostat turned the furnace on.

I remember thinking, "Boy, that would be nice, but the gas is off so this will just blow cold air." I stuck my hand down by the *vent to prove my own point when I realized with great celebration, "That's heat! That's warm air!"* I didn't want to run the battery down, but I let the furnace run for a few minutes to heat up the cabin before turning it off, rejoicing that while I didn't have enough sense to turn on the heat - Eddie did.

I awakened at 4:00 a.m., and by 4:30 a.m. I was on the road, heading east on I-78 toward New Jersey. After the engine began to heat up, I reached up and turned on the heater (the one that runs off the engine). Now, as I prepared Eddie for our trip south to Florida, the *heater* was the furthest thing from my mind. I mean, after all, who needs heat in Florida? The better question might have been, "Who needs heat in Pennsylvania in mid-October?" I had never turned the heater on and when I did, on that frosty October morning in Allentown, Pennsylvania, I waited for heat that never came. As my frosty breath was clouding up the windshield I thought, "Great, I can't wait to get to Vermont."

By sunup, I was in Suffern, New York and the New York Thruway. I had to stop for gas, of course, and was delighted to find that mid-grade Sunoco gas on the NY Thruway was selling for a mere $3.09 a gallon. I filled up the 40-gallon tank and headed north again. By that time, thankfully, the sun was beginning to heat up the air and I wasn't suffering quite so much. I pulled into our driveway at 12:30 p.m. on Tuesday, October 17, shifted the gear lever into Park, shut the engine off with a sigh of relief and Eddie's Great Adventure officially ended.

Eddie sits quietly in front of my workshop now as we gradually unpack everything, drain the water lines, put antifreeze in the lines and do some minor repairs.   Soon, I will put a cover over Eddie and bed him down for the winter. A lot of decisions will need to be made before next spring.

Will we keep Eddie and risk another adventure? There are a lot of folks suggesting I sell Eddie and get something newer, sleeker, and *easier*. I think to myself, "Where's the fun in that?"

I don't know that I will ever do a trip as long and hard as Vermont to Florida again with Eddie. I really, really doubt it. However, we do like Cape Cod and we travel to Amish Country a lot. I am thinking we'll just keep the old boy for a while. He might just have another adventure or two in him. I know I do.

After all, *what could go wrong?*

Made in the USA
Columbia, SC
03 March 2019